Kwok Nai Wang

A CHURCH IN TRANSITION

A CHURCH IN TRANSITION

Author :   Kwok Nai Wang

Editor :   Lida V. Nedilsky

Published by :   Hong Kong Christian Institute
                  11 Mongkok Road, 10/F
                  Kowloon, Hong Kong
                  Tel (852) 2398-1699   Fax (852) 2787-4765
                  e-mail   hkci@netvigator.com
                  website   http://www.freeway.org.hk/hkci/

Production :   Clear-Cut Publishing & Printing Co.
                  Tel (852) 2889-6110

First Edition September 1997

Printed in Hong Kong

ISBN 962-7471-32-1

Table of Contents

INTRODUCTION

After 13 years of preparation, Hong Kong finally has been turned into a Special Administrative Region (SAR) of China. According to a survey done by the Social Science Research Centre of the University of Hong Kong conducted just prior to the changeover, about 65% of Hong Kong's citizens were not excited about this change.

Part of the reason for such lack of enthusiasm is due to the fact that almost 45% of Hong Kong's citizens are refugees of the People's Republic of China, and an additional 30% are their descendants born in Hong Kong. But more importantly, from the Sino-British negotiations about Hong Kong's future through the entire transition process, Hong Kong's citizens were never consulted nor given any significant part to play in the determination of their future. Hong Kong politics was and still is dominated by a very few people, mostly business tycoons, senior government officials, and a handful of elites.

This is a crucial time in Hong Kong's history, where concerned people should unite in their actions. Already, in the first ten days of the HKSAR, there was a rolling back of citizens' civil and political as well as economic and social rights. The new government has enacted laws inhibiting the right of citizens to speak up. It has frozen laws which protect workers' rights. It has reintroduced the appointment mechanism in the seletion of members to the three-tier council system. The poor and the powerless will suffer as a result of these moves.

As a social conscience, it is high time that the Church in Hong Kong re-examine itself. It must reassess its involvement over the past century and a half in Hong Kong's entire social process. From this exercise, it may be able to map out its appropriate role and chart a course for the future.

This book attempts to start this exercise in assessment by looking critically at the Church in Hong Kong, from its more humble beginnings to its present position of influence, giving special consideration to its historic drawbacks and its weaknesses. From this, it is hoped that the Church in Hong Kong can eventually change its conservative stance and take on a new role, one which contributes even more to the development of Hong Kong and the well-being of all its citizens.

This author is grateful to Ms. Brenda Tam, who typed his manuscript, and Ms. Agatha Wong, who assisted in the whole production process; and especially grateful to Ms. Lida Nedilsky, a doctoral student at the University of California, San Diego, who volunteered to be the executive editor of this book.

PART ONE

OPPORTUNITIES IN THE COLONIAL ERA

1. Social Services

2. Church Growth

3. Advocacy

Tracing the history of the Church in Hong Kong, it becomes apparent that there are in fact three churches and three histories which have arisen from the social context of an ever-changing Hong Kong. Although none has occupied solely any one aspect of the Church's mission as savior, provider, and educator. Yet, each has tended to dominate certain roles concentrated at various points in history, so that we can roughly place the institutional church in the realm of social service, the evangelical church in the realm of conversion, and the activist church in the realm of advocacy. Recognizing the fact that while the general mission of the Church remains timeless, it cannot be ignored that the Church must respond to the particular needs of the day. The Church of Hong Kong has exhibited this type of contextual sensitivity. But there have also been factors working to encourage conservatism. As Hong Kong faces the prospect of a new stage in its political and social development, the activism of its recent past will be its saving grace -- and the framework for a Church meant to serve the people.

1

Social Services

Mainline Churches

In terms of numbers, Christians in Hong Kong are in the minority, representing just 8% of the population (Note 1). Out of the 6.3 million citizens, about half-a-million are Christians: 250,000 are Roman Catholics while 250,000 are Protestants. Despite being an absolute minority, however, the Christian presence is in every corner of the city. There are literally thousands of individual buildings and apartments displaying visibly the symbol of Christianity --the cross. By one estimation, there are more than 1,100 Protestant congregations, and more than 100 Roman Catholic parishes and parish centres (Note 2). The churches together operate directly or indirectly half of the secondary schools in Hong Kong (around 220), 40% of the primary schools (around 250) and 30% of the kindergartens (around 280). In addition, there must be a thousand social service centres and clinics in Hong Kong managed by the churches. Fifteen hospitals are currently operated in the name of "Christian" orders. The Christian community in Hong Kong is also responsible for running a hundred para-church organizations (such as Bible societies and fellowships), and about an equal number of Christian book shops, Christian publishing houses, seminaries, and Bible schools (Note 3).

Christian churches throughout the world have always viewed educating young people as one of their missional priorities. The Church in Hong Kong is no exception. When the missionary societies came to preach the gospel in Hong Kong as elsewhere, one of the first things they did was to build a missionary compound. Within the compound, other than offices and living quarters for missionaries, invariably there was a school, and perhaps a clinic. In Hong Kong, many of these small schools became full-fledged secondary schools in later years (Note 4). In the 1950s, of the 30 most famous secondary schools, with the exception of five directly run by the government, all were run by churches or church organizations. These were classified as "grants schools." By and large these schools produced students who had good academic achievements. Until the 1960s, these schools monopolized almost entirely the admissions into the University of Hong Kong, the only university in the territory until 1962. Parents from well-to-do families employed whatever means necessary to get their children into these church-run, "elite" schools.

In the 1960s, because of the great demand for school places at both primary and secondary levels, mainline churches, which included especially the Roman Catholic Church, the Anglican Church and the Hong Kong Council of the Church of Christ in China, responded to a call for help by the Hong Kong government. The churches worked to raise a great deal of financial and manpower resources (mainly from overseas) to operate schools. The first priority was to build rooftop schools in resettlement estates (Note 5), to be followed by government-built "standard schools" (Note 6). Also, because of more urgent demand, primary schools preceded secondary schools. The Hong Kong Council of the Church of Christ in China, the third largest school-sponsoring organization in Hong Kong, managed four schools in 1960.   By 1985 the total number had risen to 64 schools --primary and secondary combined.   Today the Anglican Church has more than 100 schools, and the Roman Catholic Church 270.   Because of this partnership between the government and the Church in dealing with a shortage of schools, Hong Kong was finally able to introduce 9 years of compulsory and free education in 1978 (Note 7).   The institutional churches' efforts and contributions to providing education have been greatly appreciated by the government and the wider community.

The Church in Hong Kong has also been a pioneer in introducing many other kinds of education and schools.   The Lutheran World Service in 1961 started Pui Oi School, a school for children with multiple handicaps, and established the Kwun Tong Vocational Training Centre in 1967.   In order to help train blue collar workers, a very important labour force in a city characterized by its light industry, the Hong Kong Council of the Church of Christ in China started Kei Heep Prevocational School in 1963.   This was the beginning of non-traditional book-learning education in Hong Kong. Before that time, every family wanted its children to have a standard education.   New immigrants from China especially believed blue-collar workers had no future; only white collar office jobs would be good enough.   For this reason, and despite the fact that their children were not suited for the education provided, they insisted that their children should at least complete the secondary level in the regular grammar schools (Note 8).   Over a decade later, however, parents finally came round to recognizing that a better alternative did in fact exist for preparing their children to enter Hong Kong's working world. This alternative existed because of the Church's involvement in the area of education.

Another very significant contribution made by the churches in Hong Kong has been in the area of medical services.   The Alice Ho Mui Ling Nethersole Hospital, the first full-fledged general hospital in Hong Kong, was organized by the London Missionary Society in 1887. Later, it became a teaching hospital.   The father of modern China, Dr. Sun Yat-sen, was one of its outstanding students.   After the turn of the century, the Roman Catholic missionary societies organized at least seven hospitals (most of which today are private). The Adventists were another major hospital-sponsoring body in Hong Kong. In the 1960s, Protestant churches (mainline and evangelical alike) worked together to build the United Christian Hospital. The hospital would come to epitomize outreach and accessibility as it pioneered the concept of a community hospital in an industrial area in Kwun Tong, and championed the idea of a hospital without walls. In 1973 it would begin operating a community health project.

Because of intense need, many overseas evangelical missionary societies in the 1960s and 1970s also started running both general clinics and dental clinics to serve the local population.

Emergency relief was yet another aspect of social service the Church was to take on. As a result of the communist assumption of power in mainland China in 1949, hundreds of thousands of people poured into Hong Kong between 1949 and 1954. According to government reports (note 9), there were some 600,000 people living in Hong Kong in 1946. Just ten years later, there were 2.5 million. These refugees, or "new immigrants" as they would later be called, were in urgent need of shelter, food and clothing. Missionary societies, forced out of China in 1949 and 1950, contributed a great deal of financial and human resources to provide the necessary assistance. Temporary homes were built (Wesley Village and Asbury Village, built by the American Methodist Church, being two good examples). Relief was provided. Rice, noodles and canned food, especially milk powder, were given to all those who required it. Later, scholarships were given to thousands of promising young people, many of whom have since become highly successful professionals and academics both in Hong Kong and abroad.

The Hong Kong Christian Council, organized in 1954 by the mainline Protestant denominations, played a key role in coordinating all the relief efforts given by churches, locally as well as overseas. In the 1960s and 1970s, Caritas, Lutheran World Service (Geneva-based), and Church World Service (New York-based) (Note 10) --the biggest social service providers in Hong Kong-- pioneered a score of new services. Ranging from child care to hostels for the elderly, and from foster care to counselling, they were designed to meet the increasingly crucial individual and social needs of Hong Kong's residents. After the riots in 1967, in order to address the needs of young people, the "tea house ministry" was founded. Youth service, including centre-based youth work, outreaching, and school social work, was to become one of the most important developmental social services in Hong Kong. Today, youth workers from many Asian countries come to Hong Kong to learn the delivery model of these services.

In summary, local churches came to be and are today the biggest social service providers in Hong Kong. By one count, they are responsible for at least 40% of the high schools, primary schools and kindergartens, 20% of the hospital beds, and more than 60% of the social work-related services in Hong Kong. Without these services, clearly, few if any citizens at the bottom of the social ladder (particularly new immigrants from China finding themselves in a society where government maintains a distance from social concerns, and lets the laws of the market decide people's fates) could have risen above the poverty in which they were mired.

Influence and Privileges

How did the Church in Hong Kong come to take on such a broad yet deeply entrenched role, ensuring the vitality and viability of the local community?

Hong Kong Island was occupied by the British military in 1841. Immediately thereafter, the Christian Church began working in the territory. First came the British military chaplains (from the Anglican Church and the Roman Catholic Church). Soon these chaplains also ministered civilians. The work of the Christian Church was greatly assisted by a Christian, if not God fearing, colonial administration. All 28 governors in Hong Kong were at least nominal Christians, while the last and former Governor of Hong Kong, the Right Honourable Christopher Patten, is a devout Roman Catholic.

Also worth mentioning is the tacit church-state relationship existing in the United Kingdom, and introduced to Hong Kong once the territory was officially established as a British Crown Colony in January 1843.   The Queen of England is still today the nominal head of the Church of England.   Her government is duty-bound to appoint the Archbishop of Canterbury, the head of the Anglican (Episcopalian) Communion throughout the world.   Several senior bishops are members of the House of Lords.   Similarly, in the Church of Scotland (Presbyterian) as well, the Queen serves as symbolic head.   At the assembly hall of the Church of Scotland in Edinburgh, the royal box occupies the space above the moderator's chair.

This highly visible church-state relationship was, as mentioned, carried over into Hong Kong.   In the protocol list of the Hong Kong government, the Anglican Bishop and the Roman Catholic Bishop have (at least up until the handover) been traditionally placed in the fourth highest position, just behind the Commander of the British armed forces, the Chief Secretary and the Chief Justice; and before the Senior Member of the Executive Council and the Senior Member of the Legislative Council.

Once the official churches of the colonial power were ensconced, their presence and functions paved the way for others to come. Following in the footsteps of the Church Missionary Society (Anglican) and London Missionary Society (Reformed and Congregational), many other foreign Christian societies also sent missionaries to Hong Kong.

The Reverend K.F.A. Gutzlaff, a Lutheran, came to Hong Kong in November 1843, and worked as an assistant to the governor.   At his invitation, the Barmen Missionary Society, the Berlin Missionary Society, and the Basel Missionary Society started to send missionaries to work in Hong Kong in 1847 (Note 11).

Before the 1970s, the two bishops in Hong Kong, especially in the persons of Bishop Roland O. Hall (1934-1966) and Bishop Lawrence Bianchi (1952-1968), were extremely influential. Indirectly they started many different types of social services in Hong Kong. They also exerted much influence on senior civil servants through personal contacts or ministries to their families. Mustering a great deal of support from the government for the work of the Church in Hong Kong, the bishops' successes reflect the closeness possible between the Church and the state under the British colonial system.

The most valuable assistance the government gave to the churches in Hong Kong was through its granting of public land. The Anglican St. John's Cathedral is the only piece of freely-held land in the whole colony of Hong Kong (Note 12). A lot of very valuable land was leased to churches for specific purposes (e.g., the building of churches, schools, and social centres) either at nil or at an extremely low premium. Consequently, the Roman Catholic Church, for instance, today owns numerous valuable properties on Hong Kong Island, Kowloon Peninsula and in the New Territories. In Kowloon Tong, La Salle College, Maryknoll Convent, and Maryknoll Convent School occupy a whole block starting at the corner of Waterloo Road and Boundary Street. On Waterloo Road in Yau Ma Tei, there is the famous "holy mountain." It is the site of Wah Yan College, Kowloon, the Lutheran College, Kowloon True Light College, the Lutheran Centre, the Truth Lutheran Church, the Tao Seng Christian Publishing House, Ward Memorial Methodist Church, and the Yang Social Service Centre.

As a result of past arrangements with the government, many churches and church organizations have recently become extremely wealthy reselling prime real estate to property tycoons. In 1992, the Council for World Mission (formerly the London Missionary Society) moved its Nethersole Hospital to Tai Po, and sold the Mid-levels site for HK$1.68 billion. The American Baptist Convention sold six pieces of property in Kowloon Tong, fetching HK$460 million.

Churches continue to benefit from a somewhat private arrangement with the government.   In May 1981, as a result of an earlier meeting between the Chief Secretary, Sir Jack Cater, and two bishops (Bishop Gilbert Barter and Bishop John Baptist Wan) and the General Secretary of the Hong Kong Christian Council, the following agreement was reached (subsequently passed by the Governor-in-Council):

> Religious bodies may be granted land at nil premium:
>
> a)   for the purposes of divine worship, provided that the premises normally occupy no more than one floor of the social services building and are also used for community uses compatible with their religious function; and
>
> b)   for a priest's/supervisor's quarters, provided that this does not exceed 200 square metres gross floor area and that a substantial part of his duties is associated with the social service purposes of the building.

The Executive Council also noted that the proposed new policy would not benefit smaller religious organizations unable to provide social service facilities, or those which concentrated mainly on evangelical work.   But individually they could be assisted by a continued sympathetic approach on the part of the Housing Authority and the Administration as in offering the use of community and school halls on a non-exclusive basis.   It has, therefore, been proposed that in future, applications should be entertained strictly on the basis of their own merits.   Religious bodies wishing to use such halls in either aided or government schools, not just for religious services (the congregation for which need not be restricted to staff and students) but for related religious activities, can do so, provided that no interference is caused to the operation of the educational facilities.

The mainline institutional church leaders have been both powerful and influential in Hong Kong.   Not only have they acted as anointed leaders of the local religious communities, but they have also managed a huge social service empire in the territory. The institutional church in Hong Kong is the second biggest local employer. It provides jobs for thousands of teachers, social workers, nurses, doctors, clerks and secretaries (Note 13). With few exceptions church leaders sit on school boards and management committees, having the final say on appointments of new staff and the promotion of serving staff members, as well. In Hong Kong, jobs in the government-subvented (subsidized) institutions offer generous pay. Differences in salary between each grade is, moreover, phenomenal. For instance, a principal of a high school earns seven times as much as a junior teacher. Likewise, a teacher earns at least twice as much once he or she is promoted to the rank of senior teacher.

Church leaders are influential also because a great many of their lay supporters are senior government officials, successful professional people, or businessmen and businesswomen. Many of these are graduates of the so-called "elite" schools run by the churches. They have considered it beneficial to have close relationships with church leaders or even pastors, since the religious leaders never challenge what they do but are only too willing to give them the kind of spiritual support and friendship they need.

Dependency Syndrome

On the face of it, the mainline churches in Hong Kong have done a lot in providing social services to the needy throughout the colonial era. Undoubtedly this will continue even though Hong Kong rejoined China on July 1, 1997.

Yet, as far as the provision of social services is concerned, the local churches in Hong Kong have never been the real masters of their own houses. Their ability to offer assistance, and their apparent resultant power gained from the control over and the profitability of these ventures, masks an underlying weakness rooted in long-established dependency.

In the early days, the missionary societies wielded the actual authority.   The famous hospitals and schools were all missionary hospitals and missionary schools.   With missionary societies coming to Hong Kong to set up their projects, local churches were used for the purpose of having local contact persons.   Actual power lay with the senior representatives of the missionary societies.

The 1960s heralded the movement of indigenization.   Local churches decided they should aim to self-support, self-govern and self-propagate.   This wave of indigenization was purely a reaction to over-dominance on the part of senior missionaries (labelled "old hands").   Indeed, church leaders at the time had come of age (Note 14).   But it was also due to the fact that many of the mainline missionary societies from North American faced budgetary constraints and shifts in priorities.   They could not raise as much money as they had done in the past.   Moreover, as Hong Kong was already considered an affluent region in the late 1960s, the money these societies did raise was channeled to more needy areas in Latin America, Africa and the Asian subcontinent.

Meanwhile, the mainline churches in Hong Kong sought independence from the missionary societies.   In order to keep themselves going, however, they had to rely more and more on their managing of social services.   For example, the Anglican Church had to rely heavily on its schools in annual fund-raising campaigns to support local church pastors.   The Roman Catholic Church had to rely on its social service centres to raise money yearly for Caritas, the social service arm of the church.   The Hong Kong Council of the Church of Christ in China depended on the sale of textbooks and exercise books to its 70,000 students in the 1970s to support the administration at the church's headquarters.

While the mainline churches kept on expanding their social services in the 1970s and 1980s, they had to rely more and more on government subventions or subsidies (Note 15), and contributions from the wealthy.   With the exception perhaps of its chaplainary work in schools, which was not supported with government money, the Church paid practically nothing to keep its "outreaching" work going.   Social services are terribly expensive.   Their costs are beyond the means of any church.   Considering that the regular budget of a high school today is HK$18 million a year, it is clear that churches must solicit outside funding sources to maintain their projects.

In order to see how churches have depended on the government and the wealthy, let us take the building of a church high school as an illustration.

Typically, after the government has approved a church's plan to build a high school in a designated area, it grants the church a piece of land.   It also pledges to cover 80% of the capital costs, which includes the cost to put up the building or buildings, as well as fixtures, furniture and equipment.   The church itself has to raise the remaining 20%, amounting to approximately HK$7 million.   Such a huge amount of money is very difficult to raise from within the congregation.   An easy solution for church leaders has been to ask a wealthy person or a charitable trust or fund, invariably controlled by wealthy business people, for help.   In return, the church promises to have that school named after the donor or the donor's father or mother.   As visitors go around Hong Kong today, they can see a lot of schools (and, in the same regard, social centres) named after wealthy people and/or their loved ones.

Since the mainline churches have placed the provision of social services at the forefront of their mission, and since these services are so terribly expensive, Hong Kong churches have no alternative but to rely more and more on the government as well as on the rich for support. The institutional church leaders unconsciously have been absorbed by what in Hong Kong constitutes the establishment, and thus are today a part of the establishment (Note 16).

The mainline institutional church leaders in Hong Kong have acquired an inborn "dependency syndrome" --born of the Church's dependence first on missionary societies, and later, in the past 20 years, the government and the wealthy.   This "dependency syndrome" is very damaging to the Church's development.   Strictly speaking, it has never developed its own thinking and theology.   Before the 1970s, church leaders, mostly trained overseas, relied heavily on Western theology.   Nowadays, they look at issues from the perspective of the powerful.   Lacking original ideas of their own, they depend on "foreign" ones.

Young Christians have often complained that their pastors only act as "obedient servants" to the elders, deacons and wealthy members of their own congregations.   But would it be the fault of the seminaries that instruct and produce Christian leaders?   To some extent, arguably.   Seminaries in Hong Kong, under the influence and pressure of the institutional church leaders, have never taught their students to think independently: to stand up and say "No" to those in authority.   As a result, the majority of Christians in Hong Kong, in the same manner as the majority of citizens in Hong Kong, have acquired "weak knees."   For them it is far too easy to kowtow to people who have status, money or influence.   The general attitude towards authority is dependent and subservient.

Church leaders, and in many instances local church pastors as well, spend enormous amounts of time managing the mammoth social service empire.   Weekly, if not daily, they use up hours running around attending management meetings and committee meetings, interviewing new recruits, and signing cheques, letters and documents (Note 17).   They can hardly spare a moment to read, to study, to reflect, and --most important of all-- to map out directions for their churches and nurture their members.   Preoccupied with management, they become dependent on busy work for a sense of their accomplishment.

Furthermore, church leaders in Hong Kong have been besieged by the mind-set of expansionism.   In order to be good stewards, in their perception, they must build more schools, more social centres.

Consequently, they have only made decisions based on whether the actions undertaken would enhance their influence.   They have moved further and further away from the idea of the Church as a servant of the Lord.   Instead, they have shifted towards a dependence on worldly standards to determine the nature of their work and measure the degree of their success.

The mainline churches in Hong Kong have today become very secular and very much involved in society.   At the same time they have lost the sense of transcendence.   As a result, they now completely conform to this world's value system, and are thus unable to transform it.   The bishops could use their influence to discuss with top civil servants key issues affecting the livelihood of the masses.   But they do not do so.   They instead use their influence for self-gain.   One would expect since they are responsible for running a good portion of the social services in Hong Kong, they would offer significant input whenever social service policies are being formed.   Again not so.   One senior civil servant made it known that although the government repeatedly tried to solicit opinions from the churches about policy changes, it usually got a lukewarm response.   Another well-known educator commented that during the drive towards using the mother tongue as the medium of teaching, he had hoped the churches in Hong Kong would lead the fight.   The churches' nonchalant attitude, rather, caught him by surprise.

Church leaders in Hong Kong have often argued that the social services they provide serve the wider community well.   But the fact of the matter has been that social services these days rely heavily on the professional administrator and instructor.   It is therefore extremely difficult to nurture the Christian spirit even in a Christian centre or in a Christian school.   There is little difference between a school run by a church or a school run by a clan association.   Oftentimes, the latter actually has greater financial resources and thus provides a school that is better equipped, for the business tycoons who sit on its management committee are willing to give generously.

Mainline churches by and large have benefited under the colonial system.   In return, they have been quite comfortable in giving their support to such a system.   The colonial system basically has been a highly elitist system.   But who produced these elites?   The church-run "elite" schools should definitely assume some responsibility.   Over the past hundred years, these schools have helped train thousands of promising youngsters to study hard and to be obedient.   After graduation, these youngsters continue to work hard, never questioning those in authority, and dutifully climbing the social ladder.   With a bit of luck, many of them have reached the top rung of this ladder.   Like members of the Church's ruling hierarchy, these business and community leaders (many of whom are Christians) have been in favour of maintaining the status quo.   This, even though deep down in their hearts they have known such complicity to be far from ideal and humane.

NOTES

1. The majority of Hong Kong's citizens do not follow strictly any one religion, such as Buddhism or Islam. It is also difficult to estimate how many are Buddhists, since Buddhism is not an institutionalized religion, like Christianity. Christians usually join a local congregation, making it fairly easy to know how many Christians there are in Hong Kong. There are perhaps a few thousand Muslims. Although unaffiliated with any particular religion, many Chinese do, however, still practise ancestor worship. "Folk religions" have become an interesting area of study in recent years.

2. Over the years, Hong Kong Christian Council, the Hong Kong Church Renewal Movement, as well as the Hong Kong Diocese of the Roman Catholic Church have conducted surveys on the number of churches and church organizations in the territory.

3. Please refer to the Annual Reports published by the Hong Kong government.

4. These included, for instance, Ying Wa College (1892) and Ying Wa Girls School (1900) started by the London Missionary Society; St. Paul's College, St. Paul's Boys' and Girls' School, Diocesan Girls' School, Diocesan Boys' School, St. Stephen Girls' School and St. Stephen Boys' School, started by the Anglican Church Missionary Society; Wah Yan College Hong Kong and Wah Yan College Kowloon by the Jesuit Society; La Salle College and St. Joseph College by Brothers of the Christian Schools; Maryknoll Convent School and Marymount School by the Maryknoll Sisters of St. Dominica; and St. Paul's Convent School by the Sisters of St. Paul De Charters.

5. When the soldiers loyal to the Nationalist Party fled the mainland in 1949-50, they built their squatter huts at Rennis Mill in Junk Bay. Thousands of civilians also fled and became refugees in

Hong Kong.   Sixty-thousand built their shelters in Shek Kip Mei, Kowloon.   On Christmas Day, 1953, a fire burnt down the whole area.   In response to the emergency, the Hong Kong government rebuilt H-shaped houses in Shek Kip Mei, first six-storeyed, later seven-storeyed.   Rooftops were used as classrooms for church-run primary schools and kindergartens.   Shek Kip Mei became the first resettlement estate in Hong Kong, with its emergency dwellings managed by the Resettlement Estate Department. Not until the late 1970s were they to be replaced by public housing managed by the Housing Authority, and the primitive roof-top schools replaced by "standard schools."

6.   "Standard schools" were built by the Hong Kong government, but managed by churches or other voluntarily agencies.   As a rule they had 24 classrooms, accommodating 24 classes in the morning and another 24 classes in the afternoon.   Primary education in Hong Kong has been half-day or bi-session. Gradually, in the 1990s, however, they are being replaced by full-day schools.

7.   The Hong Kong government had at one time planned under Governor Murray McClehose that by 1991 Hong Kong's citizens should enjoy 11 years of free education.   Unfortunately this has never materialized.

8.   Before the 1960s, the education system in Hong Kong was British: six years of primary schooling, five years of secondary schooling, two years of matriculation, and three years of university (in arts, science and engineering).   The Chinese University of Hong Kong, which came into being in 1962, offered basically four-year degree courses.   Today all six universities have been forced to go back to three-year basic programmes, with the exception of medicine, dentistry and architecture.

9.   The Hong Kong government has since 1946 issued an annual report, both in English and Chinese.   It is always informative.

10. In 1976, the Lutheran World Service and the Church World Service merged with Hong Kong Christian Service. Hong Kong Christian Service has since become a very important social service agency in Hong Kong, second only to Caritas of the Roman Catholic Church.

11. The Barmen Mission helped start the Rhenish Church in Hong Kong; the Basel Mission, the Tsun Tsin Church; and the Berlin Mission, the Evangelical Lutheran Church. Please refer to Rev. Li Tze Kwong's work, in Chinese, *Stories of the Churches in Hong Kong,* Joint Publishing (HK) Co., Ltd., 1992.

12. In theory, all land in the British Crown Colony of Hong Kong belongs to the Crown (or the British Monarch). Land is therefore only leased out for a certain period of time, for example 99 years.

13. The Hong Kong government is the biggest employer in Hong Kong. There are about 180,000 civil servants. Church-run hospitals, schools, social centres, and study rooms employ no fewer than 100,000 workers.

14. The leading voice came from the Reverend Dr. Peter Wong, the General Secretary of the Hong Kong Council of the Church of Christ in China.

15. In Hong Kong, the government has encouraged voluntary agencies (the Christian Church is by far the biggest) to run schools, social centres, hospitals, and the like. As long as an agency is willing to do the things the government wants, it will be supported almost fully through a subvention scheme. The rest of the support comes from fees charging, grants from the Community Chest, or donations.

16. Emily Lau, the most popular elected legislator in Hong Kong since 1991, wrote an article entitled "An Unholy Alliance" when

she was the Hong Kong correspondent for *the Far East Economic Review*. In this article, which appeared in the December 24, 1987 issue, she outlined the behaviour of the institutional church leaders in Hong Kong. The alliance of power formed between the church leaders, business leaders and the Chinese government Lau labelled "Unholy."

17   For three years, this author was the supervisor of 16 secondary schools. He spent, on average, half-an-hour, twice weekly, just signing cheques and documents. He could never afford the time to go through any of the supporting documents.

2

Church Growth

Conservative Christians

Christians from the major denominations in Hong Kong have often complained that their leaders, both from the head office and within their own congregations, spend far too much time managing institutions and programmes (especially relating to schools), and too little time evangelising. An associate general secretary of one major denomination said that she regularly spent hours attending school functions (her church runs more than 70 schools). The agenda of the executive committee of the same church, meeting monthly, was usually loaded down with items relating to school and in-house matters.

Most of the congregations in Hong Kong, including mainline ecumenical and fundamentalist evangelical alike, are very much "evangelistic oriented." To them, the mission of the church is evangelism pure and simple, and Christians should devote all their energy and time to the pursuit of spreading God's message, gaining converts.   To the vast majority of Christians and churches in Hong Kong, evangelism is synonymous with church growth.

While the mainline congregations, especially those dominated by their headquarters (take for example the Anglicans), are fairly drab, congregations less tightly controlled by their headquarters can be quite vibrant.   The Hong Kong Council of the Church of Christ (CCC), for instance, in 1986 reported that the church had about 21,000 members in its 30 congregations.   By 1996 the membership had increased to 23,395 (despite losses due to emigration), and the number of congregations had risen to 38.

Rapid membership growth of the Christian community in Hong Kong has happened twice: once because of the influx of refugees from China in the 1950s, and again in recent years, likely due to the 1997 issue.

Before the Second World War, the pace of life in Hong Kong was slow, as was the pace of development of the Christian churches.   At the outbreak of the war, there were fewer than a hundred congregations and parishes.   Ever since the beginning of the 19th century many overseas missionary societies had indeed come to work in this part of the world.   Yet China was the primary attraction.   It was considered the most important mission field in the world (Note 1). In sharp contrast, Hong Kong was never considered an appealing mission field.   Rather, its importance lay in the fact that it was (and still is) the stepping stone into China.   So, for years before the war, missionary societies used Hong Kong largely as a key support place for their missionaries in China.   They also used it as a location for rest and recreation to benefit their missionaries who worked in China. Even today, we can find evidence of missionary homes or camps on Cheung Chau Island and the Lantau Peak on Lantau Island.

The first surge in the number of Christians came in 1949, and continued periodically in subsequent years.   Thousands of people fled the mainland after the Chinese communists secured control of the country.   Presumably, out of roughly 1.5 million refugees who came to Hong Kong between 1949 and 1956, around 50,000 were already Christians.

In the early 1950s, the missionary societies who were forced out of China temporarily, put a great deal of their resources into aiding the refugees in Hong Kong.   Refugees in Hong Kong at the time typically sought out churches to get relief, largely in the form of basic foodstuffs. Because of these contacts, many eventually became Christians.   They were known as "Rice Christians."

Church growth in the 1960s and 1970s experienced a slow down. This was mainly due to the fact that major churches in Hong Kong at that time turned their attention to operating all kinds of social service projects.   But since the 1980s, because of a new impetus given to church growth, with the exception of a few very established churches, there has generally been an increase in both the number of congregations as well as the number of individual members.

Whether the increase has been due to 1997 is hard to say.   One thing is for certain: because of 1997, thousands of Christians opted to emigrate, mainly to Canada, Australia and the United States.   But on the other hand, many more people had to face 1997 in Hong Kong, and in joining a church they likely sought special spiritual guidance to deal with their situation.

Evangelical churches --particularly the Baptists, the Alliance Church, the Evangel Church and many independent congregations-- decided to step up their efforts on "evangelistic work" as a major 1997 strategy.   It was also true that the 1980s was the era in which to reap. After 30 years of expansion in school education by the churches in Hong Kong, Christian schools had become a huge mission field. There are currently about 600,000 young people enrolled in schools run directly or indirectly by churches in the territory (Note 2).

Planting new congregations in new towns in the New Territories has become the most important work in the evangelical-oriented congregations.   Using the "split" or "amoeba" reproductive method, they usually open a kindergarten, a study centre or a youth centre in a new town, send several families to go there on Sundays, employ a preacher, and then start public worship.   This is often followed by the establishment of a youth fellowship, Sunday School, or some other para-church organization.   Later, the congregation will likely work to raise some money to purchase an apartment nearby so that they have at least a permanent office or fellowship hall.

Congregations, or sometimes the para-church organizations which they support, also evangelize in Christian schools (Note 3).   By and large, mainline churches have been keen to run schools, but have been less interested in evangelizing students.   On the other hand, evangelical churches have run only a few schools.   But they have been very keen on doing evangelistic work there as in other schools, wherever opportunities lay.   With this spirit, they have also seized every chance to work on college and university campuses (Note 4).

A lot of the congregations in recent years have pushed extremely hard for personal evangelism.   Obviously this kind of personal contact has been a highly successful tactic in coaxing friends, relatives and neighbours to come to church.

Peace Evangelical Centre (in Chinese literally Peace Gospel Church) is a typical success story of personal evangelism.   A preacher started a meeting group in a squatter-hut in 1961.   It had a rough beginning.   In 1962 alone, the premises were destroyed twice: once by a typhoon, and the other time by a squatter hut fire.   But, as a result of the dedication and diligence of its members, in 27 years' time (1963 - 1990) the Peace Evangelical Centre developed 19 congregations. It now has its own church order and organization manual.

Many independent congregations have developed along the same lines as the Peace Evangelical Centre.   Their emphasis has been on personal evangelism. They often hold revival meetings. Their worship services can be reduced to a simple formula: Praise God and Listen to God's words.   In other words, most of the hour-and-a-half spent as a community of faithful is dedicated to hymn singing and listening to the preacher's exposition of the Bible.   Eagerly sharing experiences of being reborn has also been an important part of acting as a religious entity.   In fact, this has been a crucial component of members' discipleship training.

Unlike the mainline churches, who have relied heavily on the work of their leaders (especially the ordained clergy), evangelical and independent congregations have depended considerably on the laity. The laity has managed the whole church   --everything from doing administrative to pastoral work, from running Sunday schools to fellowship groups, and from conducting worship service to prayer meetings.   It has been this kind of lay involvement and participation which has brought about growth.

Mass evangelism, though never a direct way to increase church membership, has nevertheless been crucial to the Christian community of Hong Kong in terms of focusing its work and mobilizing its members to participate in a common cause.   From November 1996 to June 1997, four mass rallies were scheduled, featuring Sun Tai Ching, the Rainbow, Louis Palau and Tong Sung Wing (Note 5).   The publicity for these rallies had an impact on the Hong Kong community both within and outside the church, exposing people to the possibility of Christian community, salvation, and alternative ways of living.

In summary, the powerful publicity campaigns surrounding mass rallies have helped the evangelistic efforts by local congregations, and the work of almost 100 para-church organizations supported by these congregations.   These para-church organizations, many of whom work for specific target groups (like prisoners, students, patients and their immediate families) also publish books and produce attractive publicity materials sent regularly to congregations and individual Christians.   As a result of all these efforts, the increase in church membership has thus far offset the number of Christians who in the past decade and a half have left the territory for good.   The Hong Kong Church Renewal Movement in 1995 reported that there were 860 congregations in Hong Kong in 1989; this figure jumped to 1,056 in 1995.   There were 120,000 Sunday worshipers in 1989; by 1995 the number had jumped to 200,000 (Note 6).

The "Moral" Majority

Christians in Hong Kong are the minority despite the strong presence of the Church and its influence on society.   Roughly, there are about 250,000 Roman Catholics, 100,000 mainline Protestants, and 150,000 evangelicals.   As mentioned earlier, the total number represents 8% of Hong Kong's total population.

Overall, Christians in Hong Kong behave no differently than do most citizens: totally secular and materialistic (with the exception, perhaps, of one or two hours in church on Sundays).   Like the non-Christians in Hong Kong, most Christians have adopted the "everybody for themselves" mindset.   By and large, public affairs or social concerns are foreign considerations to the main body of the Christian community in Hong Kong.

Firstly, more than 90% of the Christians in Hong Kong are Chinese (the rest are mainly Filipinas working as domestic helpers; otherwise they are Korean, American and European business people). To respect and obey authority is very much in the Chinese blood.   As government represented the highest authority traditionally, Chinese always tried to avoid it (Note 7).   As government authorities took care of public affairs, they at the same time tried to stay away from public affairs.   China was then (as it is now) a very big country.   Since public transportation was not good, and because China was an agrarian society, the majority of its people seldom came in contact with people outside their family or beyond their village (which was in some cases made up of people from the clan, i.e., extended family).   There are two famous Chinese sayings which highlight the resultant attitude, one being, "When the sun comes out, I work; when the sun sets, I rest. When I want to eat, I plough the fields; when I want to drink, I dig a well.   The Emperor or the civil authorities have nothing to do with me."   The second one being, "Every family sweeps the snow on the doorsteps of its own house.   Never mind the heavy ice on the roof of your neighbour's house."   These sayings describe vividly the basic mindset of practically all people of Chinese blood, Christians included.

Secondly, a great many Christians in Hong Kong originally came from the mainland.   They have never considered Hong Kong as their home, having come here to make a living.   Since Hong Kong has provided them with relatively stable conditions to pursue this life goal, they have not cared to ask for anything more, even though sometimes they have not been treated fairly.

Thirdly, whether born and raised locally, or migrated from the mainland, people living in Hong Kong have been greatly influenced by its unique traditions.   Hong Kong was a British Crown Colony until July 1, 1997.   What the colonial administration did was to try to maintain strict law and order, that no one should challenge its legitimacy in governing and that its rule be smooth and efficient.   The British-Hong Kong administration was very successful in shaping its population into well-behaved and conforming citizens.   The local education system also taught students to be obedient.   The value system it tried to instill among its students was very simple: work hard and you will be rewarded.   Indeed, when students worked hard (meaning they did a good job in memorizing what the teachers or textbooks said), they could get good grades.   In turn, they would be admitted to a degree program.   If they did well in university, they would be guaranteed a good job.   Afterwards, if they worked hard in their job, they would climb a lot higher up the social ladder and earn lots of money.   In other words, young people in Hong Kong have never been taught to be inquisitive, especially in cases where queries challenged the authorities, questioned the way things were done.

Fourthly, most of the Christians in Hong Kong have never

received any Christian education.   According to one survey, 70% of the Roman Catholics participated in no church activities besides Sunday morning or Saturday evening mass.   Even for those who cared to take part in any education programme, their outlook would not be broadened very much.   The Christian teaching in Hong Kong has failed miserably in assisting the Church to relate to society.   As a matter of fact, Christians in Hong Kong do not know how to relate the Christian faith to their daily living.   Not too long ago, the author of this book was invited to lunch after a Sunday service.   An elder of that church who was not present at service arrived after everybody had sat down.   Obviously unaware of the presence of an ordained minister, he asked another elder, "How were your horses last night?" (Meaning, how did he fare in his gambling on Saturday evening.) Immediately he was shut up: the guest preacher was duly introduced, and the topic of conversation changed.   To most Christians, faith has no life implications.   Few are able to relate together their faith and their life.

The majority of Christians in Hong Kong are middle class, consisting of teachers, social workers, white collar office workers, and the like.   Few belong to the lower class.   The Church in Hong Kong as a whole has found it extremely difficult to reach the blue collar workers (Note 8).   Although blue collar (or factory) workers have often been exploited, yet the Church as a whole has advocated support for the status quo which allows this exploitation.   In fact, the messages contained in typical sermons have not been about the good news of liberation.   Rather, sermons have tended to be lectures about how Christians should be good, adhere to the "morals" of the society, and not rock the boat.   Indeed, "Don't rock the boat, play it safe" has become the 11th commandment of the Church in Hong Kong.

In general, Hong Kong Christians and the less privileged masses have been miles apart.   "Social Justice," which the historic Church championed, and which was indeed a vital concern of the classical prophets in the Old Testament, has now become at best an empty slogan for the churches in Hong Kong (Note 9).

While the mainline denomination leaders have advocated stronger ties between the Church and the state, evangelical leaders on the whole have been reactionary. They have taken the opposite position: that the Church should stay away from the state. For years, institutions run by evangelical churches have refused to receive any government money even if it meant they would have a burdensome financial problem on their hands (Note 10). Oftentimes, this chasm between the Church and the state has been extended to constitute a chasm between the Church and the entire social-political-economic process.

Over the past one hundred and fifty years, the Church in Hong Kong has played a significant part in providing social services to the wider community, and enlisting people to become members of the Christian community. Yet, consistently, it has paid Hong Kong's deeply rooted social problems only lip service. Such an attitude calls to mind the situation when Jeremiah criticized the priests and prophets of his time, "They have healed the wound of my people lightly, saying, 'peace, peace' when there is no peace" (*Jeremiah* 6:14).

In preaching hope while at the same time refusing to look at the realities, and in admonishing its members to place their faith in the authorities when those authorities clearly took advantage of the people, the Christian Church in Hong Kong has on the whole become a negative social force rather than a progressive force within society.

Preparations for the Future

It would be difficult to assess the extent to which churches in Hong Kong prepared themselves and their communities on the eve of 1997. For most church leaders, lay and ordained, the change of sovereignty was too big a political issue for them to handle. Worse, many did not want to even talk about it openly, much less to deal with it seriously, simply because they considered it a controversial issue.

Many Christians, viewing the world from the pew, expected

guidance from their leaders.   Others hoped that at least churches in Hong Kong should work together in facing a stark future.   As a rule, they were all disappointed.   Just within the eight-month period of November 1996 to June 1997, there were four large-scale mass crusades. Many pastors complained that it was difficult for them and their members to organize support.   Highly competitive and adversarial, these crusades for Christ forced a free-for-all situation.   Consequently, none of the crusades yielded good results.   Church leaders in Hong Kong were exceptionally quiet during Hong Kong's journey to the 1997 handover; they continue to do their own thing rather than finding new ways to work together.

There are now 17 seminaries and Bible schools in Hong Kong. Every denomination has demanded it have its own.   As a result, resources have been spread so thin that no one is well equipped and supported.   It would be expected that in facing serious challenges they would cooperate much more than before, and that their supporting churches would work harder to draw up plans for merger so that resources could be pooled together and better utilized.   Such an outcome has not yet materialized.

Superficially, churches have worked together at the congregation level through the Hong Kong Chinese Christian Churches' Union (HKCCCU).   Founded in 1915, it represents about one-third of the congregations in Hong Kong.   Its most important work has been the management of Christian cemeteries, from which the HKCCCU reeps huge profits.   Unfortunately, few church leaders are interested in it, and it has been in danger of becoming an ineffective and inward-focused social group.

Mainline denominations have also worked together through the Hong Kong Christian Council (HKCC).   Founded in 1954, it champions itself a social pioneer.   Few denomination heads have been actively involved in it.   But at least member denominations have been happy to delegate certain functions to the HKCC, functions such as: a) doing the things which denominations find inconvenient to do, and b) doing the things which individual denominations are unable to do. The launching of the controversial Christian Industrial Committee in 1967 is an example of the former; and the planning and construction of the United Christian Hospital (which began operating in 1973) is an example of the latter. But since 1987, denomination leaders have decided that the HKCC can only do the things which they officially approve. This has jeopardized the "Joint Action for Mission" concept, rendering "Church unity" an empty slogan. Both HKCCCU and HKCC have been extremely silent in addressing the 1997 issue.

With the present atmosphere of self-centredness, many are afraid that if the authorities applied pressure on the Christian community, what happened according to chapter 13 of the Gospel of *John* (Note 11), and happened time again in Eastern Europe and in modern China, could very well happen in Hong Kong: Christians attacking and betraying one another.

A few seminaries have seen the importance of preparing Christians to face the eventuality that Hong Kong's sovereignty goes back to China. They have been organizing courses for seminary students and extension courses for lay people. Yet the contents of most of these courses have proven to be empty, lacking relevance to the real situations in which people find themselves (Note 12).

When several years ago *the Far East Economic Review* interviewed a denomination head on how he would prepare the members in his church, his answer was that he believed in God and that God would take care of everything. Indeed, many church leaders now admonish their faithful to pray hard. They organized a big prayer gathering in the Hong Kong Stadium (seating capacity of 47,000) on June 1, 1997, and budgeted HK$1.2 million for the event. Prayers are vital; but actions to follow-up are equally important. Without the latter, the former would be shallow and meaningless. Jesus prayed, and afterwards he went ahead to be crucified in Gogotha.

Christians in Hong Kong, like most of the citizens in Hong Kong, certainly are worried about Hong Kong's future.   Just after June 4, 1989, the Congress of World Evangelism reported that as many as one in four pastors (and preachers) was making preparations to leave Hong Kong.   Hong Kong Christian Institute did a survey in the summer of 1990, the results of which revealed that as many as one in five Christians was seeking opportunities to emigrate (Note 13).

The Roman Catholic Church conducted a survey of its own in early 1997.   According to that survey, 81.9% of the respondents said they would stay in Hong Kong after the handover; 48% said they had no confidence in China.   Half of them expressed concern about the possible abuse of power by corrupt officials, and worried about the protection of human rights in the future SAR (Note 14).

While institutional church leaders have done little to prepare their churches and their members for the changeover of sovereignty, concerned Christian intellectuals and theologians have tried their best to stir up some interest and discussion on the issue.

In May 1984, a group of Christian leaders of evangelical background issued a statement on "the guidance to Christians in a politically changing society" (see appendix 1).   In August of that same year, a group of Christian leaders assisted by HKCC published "The Manifesto of the Protestant Church in Hong Kong on Religious Freedom" (see appendix 2).   The manifesto was co-signed by 200 churches (denominations and congregations), 5 seminaries, and 44 Christian organizations.   It was presented to the head of the Hong Kong and Macau Affairs Office of China's State Council, as well as to the head of the Religious Affairs Bureau, by a group of church leaders headed by the Anglican Bishop and the General Secretary of the HKCC in September 1984.

In 1986, the ministers of the United Methodist Church, Hong Kong, issued a pastoral letter about the future of the territory.   A second one was issued in May 1997.   A group of theologians from the

Hong Kong Council of the Church of Christ in China drafted a "Proclamation For Our Times." Subsequently, it was endorsed by the church's executive committee. Overall, these documents were documents with substance. Although strategically they offered few concrete proposals, they gave important food for thought for Christians --leaders and followers alike. But unfortunately, church leaders gave little or no attention to them.

The Hong Kong Diocese of the Roman Catholic Church was by far the most progressive in terms of facing its future. In 1989, the Cardinal endorsed the "Bright Decade" document, and made it an official document of action for the entire diocese. As the decade will soon end and presumably a full report will be issued, we will be interested to see how much the Roman Catholic Church has achieved, despite the fact that it is a highly complex institution, and opinions within its community are extremely diverse.

Institutional church leaders by and large are optimistic about the future of Hong Kong. They have put a lot of their trust in China and the Basic Law. Congregations are less hopeful. Many have begun to take on the cell-group approach, starting more and more small-size congregations, house meetings, and fellowship groups. Even the Roman Catholic Church has, since the beginning of the 1990s, made the building of base communities (small, religious communities) its top priority.

NOTES

1.   Almost a quarter of the world's total population lives in China, and the country's history goes back thousands of years.   Because its great dynasties held a certain mystique and charm, a great many missionaries from overseas always wanted to live and work in China.

2.   The figure represented almost 50% of the total full-time student population in Hong Kong.

3.   Many para-church organizations provide the much needed resources (human and material) for schools, congregations, as well as their work in schools.

4.   The most prominent para-church organization to work in the post-secondary institutions is Fellowship of Evangelical Students (FES).   In 1990, this organization employed only four field workers.   Last year, their numbers were increased to 13.

5.   *The Christian Times*, in its November 24, 1996 issue (No. 482), reported that there was a great deal of overlapping in terms of organizers of these mass rallies.   Together they planned to raise HK$18.5 million, involving some fifteen thousand Christians. Due to this packed arrangement and keen competition, however, there was a big shortfall of both money and personnel.

6.   The Roman Catholic Church reported a slight decrease in the size of its membership from 270,000 in 1986 to 260,000 in 1990.   It is widely believed that it has 250,000 members now.

7.   There is a Chinese saying, "When you are alive, stay away from any government office; when your are dead, stay away from hell."

8.   Twenty years ago, when the author of this book worked in a slum

area in Shek Kip Mei, a fellowship for factory workers from the community was organized.   After two years, he attempted to merge it with the traditional youth fellowship.   Within weeks, practically all factory workers left the organization.   They found it difficult to adjust themselves to the rather middle class culture of the traditional youth fellowship.

9.   Evangelical churches have not been entirely indifferent to what goes on in society, especially when they consider certain happenings bring ill effects on the moral values which they try to safeguard.   Thus the Hong Kong Christian Council, representing the mainline churches, spoke up several times against legalizing gambling, introducing horse-racing on Sundays, selling lottery tickets in convenience stores, and setting up off-course betting stations in public housing estates.   A group of evangelical Christians started a coalition aiming to outlaw pornography. When in 1990 the Hong Kong government wanted to decriminalize homosexual acts, many conservative Christians campaigned against it.   Likewise, when a few legislators headed by Anna Wu wanted to introduce a comprehensive equal opportunities bill, they met with strong opposition from conservative Christians who looked down on gays and lesbians.

10.   Baptist University, formerly Baptist College, was an exception. For 20 years, Baptist College was a private post-secondary college. But once it wanted to expand into a full-fledged university, it had no other choice but to receive government money and be subject to its control.

11.   Chapter 13 of *John* predicted the betrayal of Jesus by his disciple Judas.   Jesus said, "Someone who shares my table rebels against me" (verse 18, quoting from *the Jerusalem Bible*).

12.   For instance, the Baptist Seminary organized a series of courses from April to June 1997 entitled "How to be citizens of God's Kingdom in the Special Administrative Region."   These were the

courses: religious sects in Hong Kong, Christian ethics, pastoral care, commentary on Romans, Exegis of Isaiah, pastoral counselling, spirituality, church music, church growth, and Christian worship.   These courses could have been offered at any place and at any time!

13.   Details of the survey can be found in Issue No. 10 of *Reflection*, a bi-monthly theological journal published by HKCI.

14.   The report can be found in the May 3, 1997 issue of *Ming Pao*, and the May 9, 1997 issue of *the Sunday Examiner*, the Roman Catholic weekly.

3

Advocacy

Issues Oriented

For the past forty years or so in Hong Kong, the mainline denominations and the Roman Catholic Church have placed a great deal of emphasis on providing social services to society's needy, while the evangelical churches have, instead, focused on church growth.   It is fairly accurate to conclude that the main body of the Church in Hong Kong has concentrated on the expansion of buildings, projects and institutions.   In other words, it has favored concrete evidence of productivity --statistics and numbers.   It has never been comfortable dealing with such abstractions as socio-economic and political issues. But it is these issues and polices which are inseparable from the actual well-being of the masses.

Oscar Romero, the Archbishop assassinated in El Salvador, reminisced some twenty years ago that when he gave the hungry rice to eat, he was hailed as a saint.   But when he asked why so many people in his country did not have enough food to eat, he was promptly branded a communist, and thus a trouble-maker.   Yet Bishop Romero's question was crucial then as it is today, for giving rice to the hungry, no matter how important, would never solve the hunger problem in the world.   The problem can only be solved some day when pertinent questions are raised repeatedly.   The Church in Hong Kong needs to follow Archbishop Romero's example and question, for instance, why, if there is so much wealth in Hong Kong (HK$700 billion has been turned over to the Special Administrative Region of Hong Kong by its predecessor), one-tenth of its citizens live below the poverty line.   It needs to question why, if Hong Kong is such a modern and cosmopolitan region, there are still so many draconian laws depriving citizens of their basic civil and political rights.

The riots in 1967 awoke not only the Hong Kong government, but the concerned people in Hong Kong as well.   Some dared to ask the pertinent questions, and then sought to deal with the problems. Questions were raised such as: Why did so many young workers feel that they were alienated?   Were they exploited by the capitalists? The Hong Kong Christian Council (HKCC) responded by founding the Hong Kong Christian Industrial Committee (HKCIC).   For the past 30 years CIC has done a tremendous job in the effort to improve labour rights and in the "conscientization" of workers about their own rights (Note 1).

HKCC has come a long way in stimulating young Christians to think and to widen their social concerns.   In the 1970 mission consultation, church leaders came together to ponder how to better equip themselves for "Joint Action for Mission."   In the mission conference in 1980, the Church turned its attention outwards. Consequently, five mission priorities were set:

a)   Evangelism among the lower-incomed
b)   Ministries to students
c)   Stronger ties with the Church in China

d) Participation in public policy making
e) Influence of citizens' value systems.

HKCC's members and staff took these very seriously. Consequently a public policy commission was created as an additional committee within the HKCC. In 1985, because of imminent changes, HKCC organized a special mid-decade mission conference. After a week's deliberations, the conference called for individual Christians as well as churches to actively participate in the drafting of the Basic Law, the democratic movement, as well as the promotion of full-scale civic education in schools. These were seen as very progressive recommendations. Yet churches and Christians should be expected to not only be socially concerned, but politically concerned as well.

Working on behalf of the churches in Hong Kong, HKCC's public policy commission was one of the most important public policy advocates in Hong Kong in the 1980s. It was one of the first local organizations to officially raise and explore the issue of 1997, arranging a seminar on the subject in October of 1981 at the Roman Catholic Holy Spirit Seminary (Note 2).

What kicked off the work of HKCC's public policy commission was the 1980 mission conference. On the very last day of the conference, citizens in Hong Kong became furious after fare hikes by Kowloon Motor Bus (franchised to serve Kowloon Peninsula and the New Territories) and China Motor Bus (franchised to serve Hong Kong Island). During the closing session conference participants resolved to ask the staff of HKCC to follow-up on this issue. In no time, the staff was able to muster the support of a dozen concerned groups. A coalition opposing bus fare hikes was formed. This saw the beginning of a brand new advocacy model, one in which concerned groups --both religious and secular, Christian as well as non-Christian-- could work together, forming an ad hoc group (usually called a coalition or an alliance).

Throughout the 1980s HKCC in general, and its public policy

commission in particular, was instrumental in creating a dynamic social movement. It took initiatives to respond to scores of social issues (Note 3), and gave a great deal of office support. Christians were especially active in the "Joint Committee on the Promotion of Democratic Government," which started the quest for direct elections in the legislature in 1986 (Note 4), and organized the Anti-Daya Bay Nuclear Power Plant Campaign (Note 5).

Unfortunately, while social movements in the 1980s were energized with vital Christian participation, they posed a serious threat for the establishment in Hong Kong (mainly business leaders and incoming Chinese officials). Consequently, institutional church leaders, who had become a part of the establishment, saw Christians rocking the boat, and decided to take action where they felt they had authority to do so.

The Anglican hierarchy attempted to still the boat by suppressing its outspoken clergy and young intellectuals. Fung Chi Wood was asked to take a study leave. A few seminary graduates were refused ordination by the Anglican Church. Institutional church leaders, who were lukewarm about the work of the council, came back one by one to sit on its executive committee, and removed all sympathizers associated with the council from posts representing their churches. Then, they decided to revise HKCC's constitution, aiming to dissociate it from the controversial Christian Industrial Committee (Note 6). But after much hustle and tussle, their efforts failed. They then resolved to have the public policy commission speak and act only when given the approval of the executive committee. This immobilized the commission entirely. For one thing, HKCC's executive committee only met every other month. It would be difficult to wait for the council's approval on most issues, for many required an immediate response. A few members resigned in protest. Not only Hong Kong, but in reality the Church itself, has become a great deal poorer as a result of these silencing measures.

The Church's silencing of Christians who played the advocacy role has created more problems within the Church than outside (Note 7). As for the social movement itself, many leaders have come of age. They have taken the initiatives. They have done the organizing. Having grown to distrust the Church's authority, while at the same time appreciating its influence, they assign the Church a minor role to play in their production, the role of a pastor. At the invitation of these activists, the former general secretary of the HKCC (as someone positioned between the Church leadership and the politicized Christian laity) has typically played this part. Whenever, for instance, a demonstration or a mass rally is being organized, he is asked to say a few words of encouragement. In the launching ceremonies of campaigns, he is asked to light a candle and to say a few sending-forth words. If the social movement needs an article from the Christian community, he is asked to contribute. Every time a key leader of the mass movement arrives at an event, this leader seeks to confirm the participation of the Church, asking, "Has the Reverend arrived?"

The turn of events at the HKCC and the mainline churches has also prompted the revitalizing of many activist groups, like the Hong Kong Student Christian Movement, as well as the launching of many new ones, for example the Hong Kong Christian Workers Association, the Hong Kong Women Christian Council, and Christians for Hong Kong Society, among others.

Activist Christian Groups

Under the protection of the colonial administration in Hong Kong, churches were able to provide a good portion of social services for the wider community. They were also able to increase their membership, expanding the number of churches when necessary and adding more local congregations and para-church organizations. Under the same administration, however, it was difficult for any organizations or individuals in Hong Kong to play the advocacy role -- at least prior to 1967. In her memoirs entitled *Hong Kong's Unsolved Injustices: The Memoirs of Elsie Elliot* (first published in The Star of Hong Kong in 1976), Elsie Elliot told about the difficulties she encountered when she tried to fight against injustices and promote the rights of the little people on the street.   Indeed, under colonial rule, police were given a great deal of power to suppress opposition and dissent.   Activists were generally labelled trouble-makers.   Moreover, there were quite a number of draconian laws in the territory, though the authorities throughout the years insisted that they invoked these laws very sparingly (Note 8).

After the 1967 riots, the Hong Kong government realized that it needed the support of the citizens, and so it hurriedly introduced a "consultative" system.   From that point up until the handover, at least, the government has used various channels to consult the general public.   The overall mood in Hong Kong has consequently grown more relaxed.   This consultative system has provided quite a bit of room for those who have wanted to advocate for social change, creating a space where government and groups can have dialogue.   In 1967, the HKCC seized the opportunity and started the Christian Industrial Committee.   Thereafter, frequent discussions between senior government officials and church leaders were held.   In 1970, the governor was invited to address the opening session of the mission conference sponsored by the HKCC (Note 9).   In 1979, the Anglican Bishop and the general secretary of the HKCC went to see the chief secretary and urged his government not to turn away any Vietnamese refugees, who at that time were fleeing to Hong Kong, arriving weekly by the hundreds.

The capitulation of the HKCC to Church authorities in the mid-1980s prompted the birth of several Christian activist groups.   These groups came into being because many Christians found the church they attended too inward-looking, dull and unconcerned (especially about social injustices).   These groups came into being also because of the 1997 issue.   Since the ratification of the Sino-British Joint Declaration in May 1985, the return of Hong Kong to China became a reality.   Many Christians felt that there were a lot of things which needed to be done to prepare their fellow Christians to face positively that eventuality.   Some of the groups organized around these concerns have concentrated on working with specific target groups and on specific issues, for example the HKCIC with workers on labour issues; the Hong Kong Women Christian Council (HKWCC) with mostly women on issues concerning women; the Hong Kong Student Christian Movement (HKSCM) with students geared at students' participation in society. Some Christian groups were based on local congregations, such as Shum Oi Church of the Church of Christian China Social Concern group, and the Baptist Mong Kok Church. Still other groups were started by like-minded Christians. The Christian Sentinels, and Christians For Hong Kong Society are two excellent examples (Note 10).

Despite the fact that these represent very diverse groups, coming from very different religious backgrounds, yet they have shared one thing in common: they have never been concerned with their own gains --economic, political or even spiritual. In fact, some members, having to live with the stigma of trouble-makers, have encountered difficulties in finding employment. For the sake of the well-being of the underprivileged, core members of these groups have been prepared to make personal sacrifices. Members of the Christian Sentinels (comprised of young, Christian professionals) and Christian Concern for Hong Kong Society (a group of college graduates of the late 1980s), for example, have not only devoted much of their spare time to work as volunteers for their respective organizations, but at the same time have for years contributed a good part of their income so that their organizations could employ staff to support their work.

Increasingly, while more and more churches have wanted to do their own thing, to organize their own mass rallies, and to run their own seminars, independent Christian groups have found common ground to work together. That common ground has not been based so much on issues --such issues as the fight for a faster pace of democratization, the struggle to safeguard human rights, or the quest to improve people's livelihood. Rather, their common ground has been their vocal opposition to authority. It has been this kind of contending spirit and courage which has bound the groups together.

These groups began with specific issues, like CIC with labour issues and workers' rights, and HKWCC with women's rights and the position of women in Hong Kong society.   But they soon found out that they could not avoid widening the scope of their missions to encompass larger concerns.   CIC has said that in order to have a meal ticket, they must also have a ballot (political decisions do influence the distribution of wealth); and HKWCC also discovered that they should be even more concerned about the general bias stubbornly rooted in the social system.

There has usually been only a handful of core members in these groups.   But most of them have been utterly committed.   Firmly believing in what they do, they have dared to challenge the point of view held by the establishment.   It has been this kind of selfless dedication which has caught the attention of the media.   Indeed, these relatively faint voices were often heard in the 1980s because of the generous coverage by the mass media, both the print and the electronic media.   As the handover drew nearer, because of self-censorship from every sector and every corner, alternative voices were given less attention (Note 11).

These groups have by no means been alone.   They have won many friends from overseas.   In fact, most of these groups have built up their own networks on the international scene.   Morally, if not financially, they have been well supported by the international NGOs.

In their struggle in Hong Kong, Christian groups have become a sign of hope not only for Hong Kong, but for people throughout the world who engage in the constant quest for the fuller realization of human dignity.

The Prophetic Minority

The Church should be a social conscience.   This was somewhat true of the Church in Hong Kong until the 1980s.   But because of the increased presence of China after the British initiated negotiations, church leaders in Hong Kong have become less confident, and hence less outspoken.   Instead, their thinking has shifted toward how best to move closer to the incoming power.   And so they have tried to erase their links with their colonial past, including ties with the colonial authorities who had given them a great many privileges and opportunities to work and develop.   From the mid-1980s on, they have been doing and saying things senior Chinese officials would find pleasing.

In the election of the Standing Committee of the Basic Law Consultative Committee (BLCC), a list suggesting CCP-approved candidates prepared by the New China News Agency (NCNA) found its way into the hands of each BLCC member.   Its discovery caused an uproar.   The NCNA later denied responsibility.   But in the meantime, the Anglican Bishop, who was on that NCNA list, came out to defend this attempt by the NCNA to manipulate elections.   Sixty evangelical Christian leaders wrote an open letter to condemn the Bishop's highly inappropriate move.   For the Anglican Bishop, however, such a blatantly political move was not an isolated incident. As one of 23 prominent Hong Kong citizens appointed by China to sit on the Basic Law Drafting Committee, he had reportedly suggested during a drafting session of the SAR's mini constitution that Hong Kong pay taxes to Beijing as do all provinces of China (Note 12). Under severe attack, the Bishop rationalized naively by saying that this was merely a gesture of patriotism.   Many other church leaders in Hong Kong have also wanted to jump on the band wagon of the pro-China camp.   This explains why on the one hand they reckoned that the provisional legislature had no legal basis, but at the same time they joined the selection committee and took part in the election of provisional legislators.

If church leaders consider that because they bear heavy institutional burdens they are not free to speak their minds, at least they should allow or even support Christians who have decided to do so.   This has basically been the model strategy adopted by Cardinal John Wu of the Roman Catholic Church.

Within the Roman Catholic Church, there are the die-hard, old "China hands," still bitter about the Communist Chinese (the reason behind why many of them had been maltreated and forced out of mainland China). Then, there are those who are pro-China and who advocate that Chinese leaders be given the benefit of the doubt, for they have had a difficult task governing such a big and complex country. Yet there are others like the Justice and Peace Commission who say that human dignity and the protection of basic rights of the little people are very important. They have not hesitated to criticize the Chinese authorities when they have violated the human rights of the masses or certain individuals in China or in Hong Kong. Basically, Cardinal Wu has permitted all these voices to be heard. In fact, the Justice and Peace Commission is an organization within the diocese and is funded by the diocese.

Christians in Hong Kong by and large have found it difficult to support Christian groups, for they have often been labelled radical. Yet the methods the Christian groups have employed to make their voices heard have, on the contrary, been extremely restrained and peaceful: calling a press conference, issuing a press statement, petitioning to certain government officials or the New China News Agency, placing an advertisement in *Ming Pao* or *the Apple Daily*, putting across their views in their publications or daily newspapers.

The reason behind the apparent blacklisting lies in the current Hong Kong reality. Nowadays, everybody wants to keep peace with those in authority. As a result, the general populace in Hong Kong may be willing to do a bit of charitable work, but refuses to support anything suggestive of rocking the boat. Rocking the boat, in the public's perception, appears to be a disruptive, a negative endeavor.

But the fact of the matter is that improvement and genuine development are only possible if criticisms are raised. For example, China, supported by the business and community leaders in Hong Kong, has said repeatedly that stability and prosperity are the most important elements in guaranteeing Hong Kong's future. In response, alternative voices have raised the question: for whom is meant this stability and prosperity? With deeper analysis, it is easy enough to see that the wealth generated as a result of hard work by all citizens has been monopolized by a few people at the top of the social ladder. When Tung Chee-hwa, the Hong Kong SAR's chief executive, put forth his plan to curb civil liberties for the ordinary citizens in Hong Kong, he promulgated the notion that there must be a balance between individual freedoms and social order. Alternative voices queried this reasoning. It has been difficult for Mr. Tung to substantiate his thinking that the more civil liberties, the less public order. On the other hand, alternative voices have convincingly argued that the more powerful the people in authority, the more powerless the citizens.

The mainstream opinion on how Hong Kong should be run can basically be reduced to the following: ordinary citizens should be quiet and take whatever is given to them, and the people with power and authority will be kind to them. To counter the increasing, though misguided, appeal of such a vision, Hong Kong needs an alternative voice. Christian activist groups, though poor in resources both human and material, have done a tremendous job in terms of being an alternative voice in the late 1980s and 1990s, and the most prominent has been the Hong Kong Christian Institute.

Hong Kong Christian Institute (HKCI) was founded in September 1988 by one hundred and twenty Christian leaders, theologians, young pastors and Christian social activists. Coming from different backgrounds --from the Roman Catholic to the Pentecostal traditions-- these people had one thing in common: they were very concerned that in this crucial period of time, there should be an effective avenue through which the voice of concerned Christians could be heard, especially when the established church in Hong Kong was so acquiescent. As put forth from the very beginning, its object has been "to gather concerned Christians together and to enable them to make a continuing contribution to Hong Kong and the Church in Hong Kong" (Note 13).

Ever since its beginning, HKCI has always assigned one staff member to support the work of the activist Christian groups and the social activist groups.   The individual responsible has done a lot of work in tasks of coordination and mobilization, although by and large initiatives still come from the groups themselves.

HKCI has been instrumental in the building of an international network for the support of Hong Kong in this crucial transitional period.   A monthly newsletter in English has been published.   Its director has talked to journalists and concerned people from overseas weekly if not daily.   He has also been happy to accept invitations to go abroad to speak about Hong Kong, its problems and prospects. All these efforts have been aimed at stirring up more interest in Hong Kong from throughout the international community.

But the most important work HKCI has done has been in the area of "conscientization."   It has published a bi-monthly theological journal entitled *Reflection* (51 have been published to date).   Over the past nine years, it has published 31 books among the following series: "Church and Society" (11 books), "Faith and Life" (12 books), "Contemporary Interpretations of the Bible" (2 books), "Civic Education" (4 books), and two additional ones on Hong Kong (Note 14).   Because of a dire need in high schools for civic education, HKCI has also published nine packages of teaching materials, each covering a specific topic, including: what is politics? what is human rights? what is democracy? what is patriotism?   These topics are deemed controversial.   Consequently, there has been next to nothing available on the market.   Study booklets have also been published occasionally for use by churches and youth centres.

Finally, HKCI has --through direct contacts by organizing seminars, forums, debates and courses-- attempted to stimulate Christians to think and to widen their concerns.   Annually, three-credit courses on how to reflect on Hong Kong's development have been offered to seminary students.   Indeed, young pastors and seminary students are the future not only of the Church in Hong Kong, but of the whole community as well.   In recent years, HKCI has also aimed to go to churches to reach young people for this same purpose (Note 15).   These feeble efforts have increasingly been appreciated. In the midst of a sea of inaction, HKCI stands as a sign of hope for people both within and outside the Church in Hong Kong.

NOTES

1.   "Conscientization" is a term increasingly popular in use among certain English-speaking Chrisitains in Hong Kong.   It refers to the consciousness-raising associated with liberation theology's methods and goals.

2.   The papers were compiled into a booklet in Chinese entitled *The Church in Hong Kong and the Future of Hong Kong*, published by HKCC in 1982.

3.   These were well documented in a book published by Hong Kong Christian Institute in January 1994, entitled *Social Movements and the Christian Church in Hong Kong - Reflections on the 1980s*.   It is in Chinese.

4.   The "Joint Committee" was kicked off by a mass rally (known as the Ko Shan Rally) attended by more than 1,000 citizens at the Ko Shan Theatre on November 2, 1986.   Subsequent rallies were held in Victoria Park in September of 1987 and 1988.   At the Ko Shan Rally, a Roman Catholic priest read the declaration; the vicar-general of the Roman Catholic Church and the general secretary of HKCC were among the ten speakers.   Seven of the ten speakers were Christians.   The "Joint Committee" constituted the most important citizens' voice in the quest to quicken the pace of democratization in Hong Kong.   Although there were no direct elections to the Legco in 1988, direct elections were finally introduced in 1991.

5.   Soon after the Chernobyl nuclear power plant accident in April 1986, China announced that it would build a nuclear reactor in Daya Bay, 40 kilometres from Kowloon.   The people of Hong Kong were astonished and shocked.   The disaster in Chernobyl was bad enough; but at least in that case the population living in the reactor's vicinity had been thin.   But Hong Kong was

densely populated. Furthermore, should an accident happen, there was no escape route (Hong Kong was surrounded by the Pacific Ocean). So, immediately a campaign was organized. The core leadership was comprised of Christians, and the spokesman was the Reverend Fung Chi Wood, Howard, an Anglican priest. Within five weeks, more than 1.1 million names were collected in a signature campaign. Unfortunately, at the end of the day, China refused to adhere to the plea by the people of Hong Kong, and went ahead with the project. But it did upgrade the safety standard of the nuclear power plant, and set up a committee consisting of citizens from Hong Kong to monitor plant safety.

6.   According to HKCC's constitution, the Hong Kong Christian Industrial Committee (CIC) is an auxiliary organization of the Council. As such, its chairperson automatically sits on the Council's executive committee.

7.   The HKCC general secretary decided to resign in August, 1988. Many concerned church leaders and theologians also left the council. Before this open schism there had been a division of labour within the church; institutional leaders managed, while activist Christians played the prophetic role. But after the mid-1980s, the break between institutional leaders and socially-minded Christians became more pronounced. This was due in large part to the fact that they looked at issues from very different perspectives. In addition, there were personality clashes.

8.   During the communist Chinese-instigated riots from May to November 1967, the draconian Public Order Ordinance, the Police Ordinance, and other restrictive laws were invoked many times. A large number of patriotic intellectuals and personalities from the movie industry were arrested and put into jail.

9. Former Governor of Hong Kong, David Trench, in an address during his term of office, encouraged the churches to do more to educate the young and to concentrate on nurturing its members, many of whom played a key role in public affairs. His speech was interpreted by some media as, "Churches, stay away from politics."

10. For a general survey of Christian activist groups in Hong Kong, please refer to *Christian Witnesses in Hong Kong*, published by HKCI in July 1991.

11. As fewer and fewer senior friends were willing to donate huge amounts of money to support the HKSCM, and as few youngsters were interested in working for it, HKSCM could not support a full-time staff. It was thus rendered inactive, as far as being an activist Christian group was concerned.

12. This could be traced to an article written by Emily Lau entitled "An Unholy Alliance," which appeared in the January 4, 1988 issue of *Ming Pao*.

13. The HKCI's stated functions are:
   To be a Christian Centre: assisting Christians to reflect on the Christian faith and to act upon it.
   To be a Forum for Christians: to share their views and experiences.
   To be a Support Base for Christians and Christian groups actively engaged in putting their faith into practice.
   To be a Think-tank: to search for directions in mission for churches and Christians, and to develop a contextual theology in Hong Kong.
   To be a Resource Centre: to interpret the Hong Kong situation to overseas Christians, and to introduce ecumenical activities and thinking to local Christians.
   To be a Sign of a continuing quest for human rights, democracy and justice.

14. The purpose of publishing these books is self-explanatory.
     They all attempted to assist Christians in relating their faith to
     their lives, the Church to society, and the Bible to the
     contemporary man and woman.

15. For a fuller picture of HKCI's work, please refer to its monthly
     newsletters in Chinese, and to its annual reports in both Chinese
     and English.

PART TWO

CHANGES AFTER THE REVERSION TO CHINA

For the Church to address Hong Kong's situation, it is necessary for it to understand what the handover has meant and will mean to Hong Kong's citizens. The coming together of two fundamentally different systems would in any case inevitably lead to some conflict and consternation. But in the case of Hong Kong, where the society has been left out of the lengthy process of negotiation and transition, the consequences are likely to be even more painful and profound. Having lived under the British with but weak guarantees of their basic rights, citizens already face a further weakening of these rights under the new administration. Moreover, the Hong Kong people ruling Hong Kong are businesspeople, individuals typically concerned with their own gains. They share with their Beijing counterparts an attitude that a smooth-running machine promises the greatest profits, and that a smooth-running machine is one that runs silently. The cronyism existing between Hong Kong's business tycoons and Chinese leaders will only aggravate the tense and precarious situation in which the majority of Hong Kong citizens find themselves.

4

China's Increasing Control

Hong Kong System Eroding

Forty years ago, Hong Kong was basically a centre for refugees. Thousands of people had fled China to come and live in Hong Kong (Note 1).   Because of a United Nations' resolution calling for a total trade embargo on China (punishing China for its role in the Korean War), being an entrepot the very livelihood of Hong Kong was severed. Who could guess at the time that after 40 years of struggle, an economic miracle would be realized on this little plot of land, only 1,086 square kilometres in area?   Who could imagine that it would ever accommodate a steadily increasing population: housing 2.5 million people in 1956, 4.4 million in 1976 and 6.3 million in 1996? Hong Kong is now one of the most modern cities as well as one of the most vibrant financial centres in the world.   The Tsing Ma Bridge (the world's longest suspension bridge) has just been opened in May 1997. A year later, the world's most advanced airport (in Chep Lap Kok, adjoining Lantau Island) will be completed and ready to serve Hong

Kong and the world.

The success of Hong Kong has been due mainly to the fact that its citizens (more than 95% of whom are ethnic Chinese) are hard-working, intelligent and adaptable to ever-changing situations both in Hong Kong as well as the world.   But the constantly self-improving system of Hong Kong has also helped.   Basically, it can be characterized as a system whereby unless situations have been out of control, the government has left the citizens alone to go on with their daily business and life.   The individual freedoms citizens have enjoyed have never been absolute, but at least by Asian standards, they could be conceived as among the best (if not the best) in the region.   Moreover, citizens by and large have been extremely well-disciplined, making them receptive to the rule of law.   The rule of law has played a dominant role in Hong Kong's success.   If in conflict, citizens have been able to rely pretty much on the territory's independent judiciary to assist them.   Since the inception of the Independent Commission Against Corruption (ICAC) in 1974, Hong Kong's civil service has been boosted, to the point where its efficiency and fairness have become world renowned.

But after Hong Kong's return to China on July 1, 1997, could the ingredients which made Hong Kong successful be maintained in tact? Unfortunately, in view of the broader transition period, there were already signs showing that Hong Kong's system would not likely be able to continue after the handover.

First of all, China promised Hong Kong "one country, two systems" (meaning the Chinese system would not come to Hong Kong after 1997, and the Hong Kong system and citizens' way of life would be allowed to continue for at least 50 years).   This promise was solemnly enshrined in both the Sino-British Joint Declaration, signed in December 1984, and the Basic Law, promulgated in April 1990.

Now that China has re-gained sovereignty, in order to maintain Hong Kong's system, China must resist the temptation to interfere in

Hong Kong affairs.   Otherwise, the Hong Kong system will be eroded and   essentially replaced by the Chinese system.   Throughout the transition period, however, it already became clear that it was far too much to ask the Chinese officials to leave Hong Kong alone.   Time and again, they wanted to intervene.   When Hong Kong decided that the existing Kai Tak airport could not accommodate the heavy volume of traffic and that a new airport needed to be built, China wanted to have the final say.   After more than a year's intensive discussion, then British Prime Minister John Major was forced in September 1991 to go to Beijing and sign the memorandum of understanding (better known as the MOU) on the building of a new airport and other related matters. The MOU effectively gave China the veto power on all Hong Kong matters straddling 1997.   Since then, China has interfered on almost every important issue or public policy in Hong Kong, such as the licensing of personal communications service, reclamation plans, the building of a strategic sewage disposal system, welfare spending, the 1996-1997 and 1997-1998 budgets, the incorporation of Radio and Television Hong Kong (RTHK) (Note 2), the building of the North-western corridor (to link the northern part of the New Territories and Kowloon), as well as the granting of building rights for Container Terminal No. 9 to a conglomerate led by the Jardine.   Without any exception, China has been successful in either stalling these plans or forcing the Hong Kong government to scrap them completely.

But even more critical is the fact that China insisted on doing things in Hong Kong according to its wishes and pleasure, rather than following the rule of law.   As a result of a number of occasions when China decided to meddle, the power of Hong Kong's rule of law has been seriously eroded.

The first occasion was the setting up of the Court of Final Appeal (CFA).   Article 82 of the Basic Law reads, "The power of final adjudication of the Hong Kong Special Administrative Region shall be vested in the Court of Final Appeal of the Region, which may as required invite judges from other common law jurisdictions to sit on the Court of Final Appeal."

China has always been afraid of having Hong Kong internationalized (meaning subject to the excessive influence of foreign powers). Not surprisingly, it forced Britain to agree to the constitution of judges in the CFA, that no more than one judge in the CFA should hold a foreign passport.

To put it very plainly, China's stipulation was a violation of Article 82 of the Basic Law. By so doing, China not only broke the Basic Law, but also threatened the independence of the judiciary in Hong Kong.

Then came the setting up of an extremely controversial provisional legislative council. This provisional legislature was not accounted for in the Basic Law. China's National People's Congress (NPC) has never taken any action concerning its setting up. So, strictly speaking, the provisional legislature did not have any legal basis. Because it began functioning in March 1997, there were laws this body enacted which preceded the handover. They are likely to be deemed illegitimate and challenged in court in the months ahead.

China has never been a great champion of democracy. So, acting on China's likes and dislikes, Chief Executive (then designate) Tung Chee-hwa announced that he would reintroduce the appointment system into Hong Kong's municipal councils and district boards. Rather than replacing popularly elected officials at these lower levels, Tung increased the total number of seats by an average of 25%. Not only did he transform the system by making these appointed positions; Tung single-handedly tipped the balance of power in favor of a particular group's interests. Thus, none of the democratically elected institutions in Hong Kong could in their entirety straddle the handover. This was a real setback for the Hong Kong system. Hong Kong has gone a long way in developing its system consistent with the many historic changes which have taken place. Because of the 1967 riots, the government discovered that it no longer could govern Hong Kong without the support of its citizens; so it introduced the whole idea of governing through consultation.

District offices and departmental advisory committees were immediately set up.   In the 1980s, because it was pursued by its citizens, the representative government concept was introduced. Hong Kong needs the participation of its citizens in all aspects, including public policy formulation, much more so now than before.

Sadly, for the past ten years China considered the British untrustworthy.   Worse still, China believed the British had conspired with Hong Kong's democratic leaders to raise havoc by introducing all these liberalizing measures.   So China made up its mind that whatever the British established, especially since 1989, China would dismantle.   That explains why China had to water down the Bill of Rights, insisted the 150,000 Hong Kong citizens who have been granted UK passports by the British Nationality Scheme of 1992 were still Chinese (and therefore not eligible for British Consular protection), and destroyed the through train in the three-tiered council system in Hong Kong which was formed by Chris Patten's constitutional reform package.   By doing that, China did little to wound Britain, which had long ago made preparations and adequate safeguards pertaining to its withdrawal from Hong Kong; but it damaged greatly the system which has been working well in Hong Kong.

China has mounted a campaign to erase Hong Kong's colonial past.   For certain, the British colonizers had not been kind to the local citizens.   Before the 1960s, Hong Kong was a corrupt and highly oppressive city.   But Britain made great efforts to improve Hong Kong's conditions.   It eventually installed a system which has made the territory a lot more modern and international.   Yes, a lot of things remained to be done and needed further improvement (e.g., the widening gap between the rich and the poor has long been an acute problem).   But for China to tear down the pillars which have supported Hong Kong's success seems totally irrational.

Obviously China wants to rewrite the history of Hong Kong. To China there are only two relevant facts: Great Britain defeated the Qing dynasty in 1841 and forced it to lease Hong Kong to Britain; 156

years later, the People's Republic of China was able to drive the British out of Hong Kong.   But is there nothing China could learn from Hong Kong, its system, and its citizens' resilience?   The citizens of Hong Kong and the people of most big cities in China enjoyed a comparable standard of living in 1949.   Why was it that after 40 years Hong Kong surged ahead, its living standard exceeding by a large margin that of Beijing and Guangzhou?

Lee Kuan Yew, the senior minister of Singapore, urged Tung Chee-hwa to scrap all of Patten's reforms in order to win China's confidence.   If Tung were to adhere to Lee's advice, it would mean the beginning of an end for Hong Kong (Note 4).

Hong Kong's system was not built in one day.   It evolved gradually and was influenced by many factors.   As a matter of fact, every system is highly contextualized.   Singapore cannot copy Hong Kong's system, and vice versa.   China's system should not come to Hong Kong; likewise, Hong Kong's system is inappropriate for China, despite the fact that they could learn from one another.

A New Stove at Work

The change of sovereignty in Hong Kong was rather peaceful. Nevertheless a realignment of the power structure was unavoidable.

The British took Hong Kong by force and established a colony on it for only one reason.   The British traders had always wanted to trade with China, already having by the 19th century the world's biggest potential market.   But as Britain was so far away, it needed a stepping stone and a supply base.   Hong Kong was ideal because of its well-protected harbour and its proximity to China.   So, ever since its beginning, the colonial administration was established in Hong Kong to serve the traders.   It had an easy task, because in the first century many Chinese came to Hong Kong to earn a living.   As Hong Kong was never considered their home, concern for public affairs was foreign to them.   Agitators could seldom get the support of the people.

Later, the colonial administration also absorbed a few of the compradores (Note 5) to assist them in ruling Hong Kong. This picture was somewhat changed after the early 1970s. Local business people had taken control of many British *hongs* (or firms), like Hutchison Whampoa, Wheelock Marden, and Kowloon Wharf. But essentially the Hong Kong government remained the same: it was there to serve the rich, and, to that effect, it was greatly influenced by the rich in its policy formulation and implementation (Note 6).

But after China's take-over of Hong Kong, the picture has been changed somewhat. The business community has stepped up its participation in government affairs. The chief executive himself is a business tycoon, as are most of his lieutenants and members of the provisional legislature.

It is ironic that China, following the path of socialism and the thoughts of Karl Marx, V.I. Lenin and Mao Zedong, would rely so much on business tycoons to rule Hong Kong. The major reason for this is that for the past ten years business tycoons have tried extremely hard to appease China's leaders. Under no circumstances would they say "No" to China.

The former New China News Agency (NCNA) director in Hong Kong, Xu Jiatun, once remarked that for the business people in Hong Kong patriotism was a matter of expediency. Indeed, years ago business leaders in Hong Kong and the leaders in Beijing formed an alliance. On the one hand, the Beijing leadership has used local business heavy-weights to act as proxies: to watch over Hong Kong and to rule Hong Kong on its behalf. On the other hand, business leaders (most of whom have vast trade interests in the mainland) have relied on members of the Beijing leadership in order to close lucrative business deals. It is worthwhile noting that in China, connections or *guanxi* (meaning, literally, relationships) are of utmost importance. Powerful people can really help you get around. Hence the more powerful people you know, the better.

It became clear that by "Hong Kong people ruling Hong Kong" (a promise by China solemnly enshrined in both the Joint Declaration and the Basic Law) China meant a highly controlled chosen group of Hong Kong citizens ruling.   This group of people might even have been pro-British before the 1980s (Note 7).   But it had since changed its stance to be anti-British.   Because China knew that this group of people had to rely on China to further its commercial interests and/or social status after 1997, it trusted it.   The group had to do whatever China wanted; or, better still, it would volunteer to carry out whatever was in the minds of the Chinese leaders.   China has used the term *aiguoaigang* (love China and love Hong Kong) to describe this group of people (Note 8).

On the other hand, China has never wanted the politicians who enjoyed popular support (or democratically elected political leaders) to be a part of the ruling clique in the future SAR.   Measures have therefore been taken, though sometimes very subtly, to eliminate most of these democratic or liberal leaders from the scene.   Indeed, the *aiguoaigang* people have been quite prepared to do the dirty work on China's behalf.   In appointing the Judicial Officers Recommendation Committee (a committee to recommend the appointment and promotion of judges) for the SAR, Tung Chee-hwa dropped two incumbent members: Sir Joseph Ho-tung and Elenor Ling Ching-man.   Sir Joseph did a "politically incorrect" thing by donating HK$200,000 to support Emily Lau, the most popular Legco member in 1996; while Elenor was a Jardine director (Note 9).   Many overseas merchants and investors in Hong Kong raised their eyebrows over this incident.   Bit by bit, Hong Kong's rather open and fair system was being taken away.

Actually, when Zhou Nan came to replace the defected Xu Jiatun at NCNA in early 1990 (Note 10), one of his jobs was to further what Xu had done (Note 11) by building in Hong Kong a new power base, known as the "second stove."

First, Zhou brought together the 40-odd traditional-style patriots who served in the NPC (National People's Congress) or the CPPCC (Chinese People's Political Consultative Conference).   This was the first batch of people to be included in the new "stove."   Next, he sought out the local talent.   Between 1993 and 1994, 186 prominent citizens of Hong Kong were appointed as Hong Kong affairs advisors (Note 12), and about 400 as district affairs advisors (Note 13).

In 1994, China decided to activate this second stove by establishing the Preliminary Working Committee (PWC).   The PWC was not accounted for in the original take-over blueprint nor in the Basic Law.   China was desperate to get the ball rolling in terms of taking over control of Hong Kong.   The PWC was charged with the task of advising and mapping out a blue print for the SAR.   As it would only do things favourable to China, it became a highly unpopular group among Hong Kong's general citizenry (Note 14).   The PWC consisted of 57 members, 27 were mainland senior officials and 30 were Hong Kong citizens.   Finally, in January 1996, in line with the provision of the Basic Law, the Preparatory Committee (PC) was established.   The PC included 94 citizens from Hong Kong out of a total of 150 members.   Qian Qichen, China's foreign minister, served as its chairperson.

In October 1996, the PC elected 400 citizens to serve on the Selection Committee.   According to the Basic Law, this committee had only one function: to elect the first SAR chief executive.   China, however, demanded that it should also elect 60 members to serve in the provisional legislature.

On December 11, 1996, Tung Chee-hwa was elected as chief executive by an overwhelming majority.   Many had predicted he would win, as he was anointed by Jiang Zemin.   On December 21, 1996, 60 members (of whom 51 were selection committee members themselves) were elected.   With the exception of two, all of them were serving members of the NPC, CPPCC, PC, or were Hong Kong affairs advisors or Hong Kong district affairs advisors.   With the advent of the chief-executive and the provisional legislature, China's building of a new power base in Hong Kong was completed. Indeed, all were Hong Kong citizens, because even those who held overseas passports had already renounced any foreign citizenship (Note 15). But when you traced the process of how they were "elected" by the Selection Committee, and recognized that the selection committee was formed by the PC, and that the PC was appointed by China, you could not very well say that these people could represent the majority of the territory's citizens. Hong Kong citizens were never given a chance to participate in any part of the political process. Moreover, the track record of the people who would rule Hong Kong indicated it was unlikely they would speak up on behalf of the voiceless among their constituents.

One Party Rule in China

By its sheer size, China is one of the most powerful countries in the world. It has more than 1.25 billion people, or about a fifth of the world's population. Its land area is 3.7 million square miles, about the same size as Europe. It is the world's second biggest economy, trailing behind only the United States. Its gross domestic product was US$3,587 billion (purchasing power parity) in 1996.

It is also the world's most powerful regime. Its military build-up and its public security are the world's largest in terms of sheer numbers. Oftentimes, outsiders link China's People's Liberation Army (PLA) with its firing on students in Tiananmen Square in the early hours of June 4, 1989. People are intimidated by the image China conjures!

It was Mao Zedong who once said that "power comes from the barrel of a gun." Indeed, when the Chinese rulers have felt their authority being threatened, they have not hesitated to use force to extinguish dissent.

As a vast country, China has been required to be extremely disciplined and vigil. It insisted on following four cardinal principles:

(a) the country had to be led by the Chinese Communist Party (CCP); (b) it had to follow Marxist, Leninist, as well as Mao Zedong thought; (c) it had to follow the path of socialism and (d) it had to have a dictatorship of the proletariat. The most important of these four principles was always the rule by the CCP. Since the inception of "modern" China in 1949, the CCP has been treated like an emperor from heaven. Nobody has ever dared to challenge the one party rule in China.

When the CCP took over rule of mainland China, the party leadership made great efforts to build up the control network, right down to the street level. Governors have been appointed in all 24 provinces; but simultaneously, party secretaries have been appointed to each province. In a university, there is a rector or president; but near his office, there is a party secretary. This arrangement of assigning a party cadre to work alongside an administrator represents the depth of party oversight not only in official but also semi-official institutions throughout the country. The power associated with such a position is recognized by those making their way up the political hierarchy.

For example, right now the head of the Chinese government is Li Peng. But Li is answerable to the Standing Committee of the party's Politburo, headed by Jiang Zemin, the party secretary (Note 16). This explains why the present mayor of Beijing, Jai Qinglin, has been canvassing hard for the position (which is held by Wei Jianxing) of party secretary in the capital. The respective party secretary holds the ultimate power, whether in the state, in a city, or in a university. By and large, it is the party secretary who makes all the key decisions; the premier, the governor, the mayor or the rector is the chief executive implementing policy decisions. The party controls tightly the state -- every province, every city, all the way down to every street. This kind of parallel arrangement of control or organization is known as the "national machine."

In China, the state is above the people, the party is above the state, and the party elders are above the party. Even in the 1980s, when China was modernizing and opening up, the country was ruled by –literally-- a handful of elderly statesmen: Deng Xiaoping, Chen Yun, Peng Zhen, Wang Zhen, Bo Yibo, Song Renqiong and Yang Shangkun (Note 17).   In other words, going back to the founding of the PRC, the rule by individual personalities and their edicts has been far more important than the rule of law.   As CCP leaders have practically all wanted to expand their power and influence, their rule has not tended to be stable, especially when they have felt insecure.

Power struggles have, however, been quite regular.   As a result, most of the good people in the party have at one time or another been purged: Chen Duxiu and Zhang Guodao in the early years, Liu Shaoqi in the 1970s, Hu Yaobang and Zhao Ziyang in the 1980s.   Deng Xiaoping himself experienced "three ups and three downs," meaning he was dismissed three times, but was able to get back to power each time.   Even Mao's anointed heirs, Lin Biao and Hua Guofeng, were unable to succeed Mao as a result of various power struggles.

In order to get rid of the party's as well as his own enemies, and thus retain his power, Mao started political movements one after the other, notably The Hundred Flowers in the early 1950s and The Great Leap Forward in the latter part of the same decade.   The most notorious one was, of course, The Cultural Revolution from 1966 to 1976.   All these political movements were extremely dehumanizing.   In order to survive, hundreds of thousands of people were forced to turn against their own family members, friends and colleagues.   Between 1958 and 1960 alone, more than 400,000 people were purged.

CCP rulers have never allowed people either within or outside the party to challenge their authority.   They have never hesitated to use the excuse of keeping the peace to crack down on dissidents.   The life of Wei Jingsheng, the most famous dissident in China, and twice nominated for the Nobel Peace Prize, illustrates vividly this kind of intolerance among top CCP leaders.

Wei was never a leader of any resistance movement in China. In 1979, he echoed the call by Deng Xiaoping, China's paramount leader, in urging that China needed to modernize its agriculture, military, science and technology, as well as economy.   But what made Deng angry was that Wei insisted on adding a fifth to Deng's four modernizations: democratization.   For his innovation, Wei was sentenced to 15 years imprisonment.   The charge made against him was that Wei had disclosed China's military build-up to its enemy during the Sino-Vietnamese conflict earlier in the year.   Because of mounting international pressure in recent years, Wei was released after serving 14 1/2 years.

Shortly after Wei was set free, however, he wrote two articles, one suggesting that Tibet should be granted independence, and the other urging the CCP to engage in political reforms in China.   He was promptly re-arrested and handed a new 14-year prison sentence (Note 18).

In China, alternative voices are not permitted.   In fact, its people are allowed little freedom.   There is little freedom of speech, freedom of the press, freedom of mobility and work.   In many provinces people are not even allowed to have more than one child in the family.   The government and the CCP are so powerful and so intolerant that they leave little or no room for the establishment of any non-governmental organizations (NGOs).   Actually, strictly speaking there are no NGOs in China.   The Chinese NGOs are in part government supported and supervised.   Even churches are highly controlled by the Religious Affairs Bureau and the Department of Public Security.

In China, those who have the power will never hesitate to use it for their personal advantage.   This is a basic human frailty. Nepotism and corruption have become extremely serious problems in China.   In the 14th Party Congress held five years ago, Jiang Zemin stated that combatting corruption was at the top of his agenda.   He even asserted that corruption was one of the most serious problems the

CCP has faced since its formation. If unchecked, the whole party and indeed the whole country would be brought down. Jiang was echoed by Zhu Rongji, China's economic czar. Zhu swore that he had prepared 100 coffins for corrupt senior cadres. In order to show his determination, he had reserved one for himself.

In the last two years, indeed, many corrupt officials have been brought to justice. The most senior ones include Chen Zitong, Beijing's party secretary, and Zhou Beifong, the general manager of Shougang, China's largest steel mill (Zhou's father was a close friend of Deng Xiaoping). But corruption is an extremely deep-seeded problem in China. For it is still a country in which the legal system has only begun to develop, and in which the rule by individual personalities is far more important than the rule of law. Hence, whether one can move around in China and accomplish a lot continues to depend on one's connections with influential officials, the higher up the better.

It has been widely reckoned that in China, the most influential group of people in business is the "princeling faction." Nobody dares touch the sons, daughters and in-laws of the elder statesmen despite the fact that they might not always conduct business in the proper way. Since Deng's death, it has been confirmed that his offspring have vast commercial interests in Hong Kong. It is a fact that rulers and senior officials of this powerful regime have amassed great power and influence, leaving the masses of people with little civil, political, economic, social and cultural rights.

Hong Kong's citizens, business people, and the men and women on the street alike are most afraid that corruption and the rule by *guanxi* will spill over now that the handover is a reality. Indeed, there are indications showing that Hong Kong's citizens have already adopted the Chinese way of doing business both in China as well as in Hong Kong.

Chinese leaders have warned their provincial officials not to come to Hong Kong to meddle in Hong Kong affairs.   But as the actions of many cadres have made clear, Hong Kong is such a fat cow that it is very difficult to resist the temptation to interfere in matters there.

Many "patriotic" individuals have argued that yes, China went through difficult times, like the political movements in the 1950s, the Cultural Revolution, and the crackdown in Tiananmen Square.   But China has learned its lessons.   China today under Jiang is very different from what it was under Mao and Deng.

Yet, as long as China refuses to give up its one party rule, the changes which have taken place will only be superficial.

One party rule is synonymous with a desire for total control. China is going to put Hong Kong under its full control.   China can use Hong Kong's business, academic, community, and religious leaders, who will remain loyal to the CCP as long as it is beneficial to themselves. China is also stepping up the CCP infiltration into Hong Kong.   The CCP's activities in Hong Kong have always been underground.   In 1982, it was exposed that NCNA had close to 400 full-time workers.   Xu Jiatun in his memoirs admitted that as chief of the Hong Kong branch of the NCNA, he had also served concurrently as the secretary of the Hong Kong and Macau working committee of the CCP.   Under his command, Xu asserted, there were 500 to 600 cadre members.   It would be extremely naive to believe that after the handover this working committee would be banned.   On the contrary, in order to keep a closer watch and thus control over Hong Kong, the CCP working behind the scenes in Hong Kong may even be more vital than before.

This is why it is wishful thinking that one day Hong Kong people may be given the opportunity to elect their own representatives to govern Hong Kong according to their own wishes.   The "two systems" concept is evaporating already.   If concerned people stay away, soon there will only be "one country," with the Hong Kong. system being absorbed totally by the Chinese system.

NOTES

1.   According to the Hong Kong government, in 1946 Hong Kong had a population of 600,000.   By 1956 it had jumped to 2.5 million.

2.   For years, the Hong Kong government wanted to incorporate RTHK, very similar to the arrangement in the United Kingdom between the British government and the British Broadcasting Corporation (BBC).   BBC, though funded by the government, is not a government agency, much less a mouthpiece of the government.   It is autonomous.   The government cannot interfere with respect to its editorial policies.

3.   The Basic Law assumed that the existing Legco elected in 1995 would continue to serve until 1999.   This explains why it says the first term of the SAR's Legco is only for two years.   From the second term on it will be for four years (c.f. Annex II of the Basic Law).

4.   Lee Kuan Yew offered his advice to Tung during his interview with the *Financial Times* on May 12 (reported by *the South China Morning Post* on May 13).

5.   Since the British traders did not know the Chinese language nor the culture, they had to rely on middle men (or compradores). Many of these compradores became extremely well-off.   Sir Robert Ho-tung and Sir Shousan Chau were two of the most famous ones.   In rendering their services to the British traders, a great many elites in Hong Kong were westernized, learning to speak fluent English, marrying the daughters of British traders, and sending their children to Britain to be educated.

6.   On paper the Hong Kong governor was the most powerful person in Hong Kong.   However, as Richard Hughes, in his 1968 book entitled *Hong Kong: Borrowed Time, Borrowed Place,*

described so vividly: the Jockey Club, Jardines, the Hong Kong Bank were ranked above him as far as power and influence were concerned.   Indeed, most of the governor's close advisors were themselves business tycoons or representatives of these tycoons. The same phenomenon appeared in Legco before 1991, when the majority of its members were appointed by the governor.

7.   The leading figures of this group included: Sir S.Y. Chung, former Senior Executive Councillor; Allan Lee, former Senior Legislative Councillor; former Legco and Exco members Maria Tam, Salina Chow, and Rita Fan.

8.   Political commentators in Hong Kong labelled them as suddenly *aiguo* people.   This group was a stark contrast to the traditional *aiguo* people.   The latter were willing to make sacrifices for China in the 1960s and 1970s.   They loved China because of their idealism and their "gut" feelings. The former group has loved China for the sake of convenience, as a way to safeguard or even enhance their vast trade interests in Hong Kong and in China.

9.   Jardine was the oldest British *hong* in Hong Kong.   It moved its headquarters to Bermuda in 1984, and subsequently delisted in the Hong Kong Stock Market.   This certainly was a sign of no confidence in China.

10.   Xu Jiatun backed the more liberal Zhao Ziyang, the former CCP chief, during the student demonstrations in the spring of 1989. But hard-liners Li Peng and Yang Shangkun, backed by Deng Xiaoping, got the upper hand.   As a result, Xu had to flee to the United States for political asylum.   Xu was the highest ranking CCP member ever to defect.

11.   Xu was a master of the "United Front" tactic.   When he arrived in Hong Kong in 1983, he spent practically all his time dining with members of the business community as well as religious leaders in Hong Kong.   His attempts to win over all the

prominent locals were highly successful.   Only a handful of liberals or democrats or more principle-minded people were unmoved by his gestures.

12.   Peter Kwong, the Anglican Bishop, and Tsang Hing Man, a vicar general of the Roman Catholic Church, were two among the appointees.

13.   Fr. Luke Tsui of the Catholic Institute on Church and Society was appointed as a district affairs advisor.

14.   It proposed, for instance, to completely derail the three-tier council system, as it was Patten's making in 1994 and 1995.   It also promoted the emasculation of Hong Kong's Bill of Rights.

15.   The declared chief executive candidates all held first class British passports -- not the second class British Dependent Territory Citizen passports as all people who were born in Hong Kong carry.   They included Lo Tak-shing (former Exco and Legco member), Simon Li Fook-sean (former high court judge), Peter Woo Kwong-ching (former Wharf and Wheelock Marden chairperson), Sir Ti-liang Yang (former Chief Justice) and the winner, Tung Chee-hwa.   Many of Mr. Tung's cabinet members, as well as the chief justice designate, Li Kwok-lan, also held full British passports.

16.   The supreme ruling body in China is the Standing Committee of the party Politburo, whose membership now consists of: Jiang Zemin, Li Peng, Qiao Shi, Li Rui Huan, Zhu Rongji, Liu Huaqing and Hu Jiantao.

17.   These eight elders all held important positions ever since 1949. But their authority came basically because they participated in the Long March in 1934 and made possible the birth of "modern" China in 1949.   As of July 1997, out of this gang of eight, only Song, Bo and Yang are still living, with both Song and Bo in poor health.

18. China may very well be the number one country in the world in terms of political prisoners in custody.   China's poor human rights record is well documented.   Amnesty International, the Jubilee Campaign, Human Rights Watch/Asia, the European Union, the US State Department, and the United Nations Human Rights Committee, which have been critical of China's human rights record, have kept dossiers on hundred of individuals persecuted and deprived of their basic human dignity.

5

Reduction of Citizens' Freedom

Curbing of Civil and Political Rights

Hong Kong was a British Crown Colony, for decades ruled by a corrupt and rather oppressive colonial administration.   In order to maintain its illegitimate authority in the territory, the colonial administration had in its pockets a set of draconian laws.   When questioned, the administration often rationalized by saying that these laws were used very sparingly.   But, in fact, during the riots in 1967 the archaic ordinance on public order was invoked time and again to put many "communist agitators" behind bars or to expel them from the territory.   In addition, several pro-China newspapers were shut down.

In her memoirs, Elsie Elliot had accounted in detail how the little people in Hong Kong were trampled on by police made powerful through an ordinance giving them broad authority.   Even today, the police can stop any passer-by and ask him or her to produce an identity card.   On a street corner in Mong Kok, it is not unusual to see police conducting a body search of a person suspected of being an illegal immigrant, of intending to commit a crime, or of having already committed a crime.   There exists the Complaints Against Police Office (CAPO), but rather than being an independent body it is actually a unit within the police establishment.

After the riots in 1967, the colonial government in Hong Kong did loosen up quite a bit.   Citizens were often consulted and even encouraged to participate in public affairs.   Dennis Bray, the Home Secretary in the early 1980s, was always very proud to say that the Hong Kong government had a dozen ways to solicit citizens' viewpoints.

To calm the citizens' nerves following China's crackdown on the pro-democracy movement in 1989, the colonial administration supported the passing of a Bill of Rights Ordinance (BRO).   It was enacted in June 1991.   But because of China's displeasure, this BRO was at best only a half-baked piece of legislation.

Basically, this Bill of Rights is copied word for word from the International Covenant on Civil and Political Rights (ICCPR); at least, that was what the government authorities claimed.   The government explained that the clauses in the other rights instrument, namely the International Covenant on Economic, Social and Cultural Rights (ICESCR), could not "be easily enforced in the courts," and therefore were not included in the bill.

When we look at the bill closely, however, we can find that there are important omissions even from the ICCPR.   For example, Article 1 states that "all peoples have the right of self-determination."   But when Britain decided to hand Hong Kong back to China, the citizens of Hong Kong were not even consulted.   This prompted Lydia Dunn, the Senior Legislative Councillor at the time, to say that Britain had only the right to hand back the land, but not the people, to China.

Article 24 of the ICCPR states that "every child has the right to acquire a nationality," but when in 1979 Britain found out that it was not realistic to keep Hong Kong, it hurriedly passed the Nationality Act of 1981, effectively taking away the rights of entry to and abode in the United Kingdom for the 3.5 million citizens who were born in the British territory of Hong Kong. The Nationality Order of 1986 further took away the right to nationality, reclassifying those 3.5 million as British Nationals (Overseas) or BNO. To many legal experts the BNO was merely the name of a passport. Britain said holders of the BNO were not British nationals, while China said they were not Chinese, at least not before 1997. Strictly speaking, all BNO passport holders became "stateless."

Article 25 says every citizen shall have the right to elect his or her own government. But Hong Kong's citizens under the British were deprived of this basic political right. The governor, who headed an executive-led government, was sent from London. He was not accountable to the local population. Until direct elections were introduced in 1991, Hong Kong's legislature was dominated by government-appointed members.

The scope of Hong Kong's Bill of Rights has not been wide enough; in fact, it is below the international standard. When the government introduced this bill, it treated it as just another piece of legislation. The BRO was not given any supremacy status. Today, consequently, it is not entrenched in the Hong Kong legal system. With the handover the new legislature can amend it or even repeal it by a simple majority vote. This is a serious possibility, considering that upon enactment of this bill China had vowed to annul it.

But the biggest drawback of the whole endeavour to safeguard citizens' basic rights has lain in the fact that the Hong Kong government refused to set up a human rights commission. Without the commission the BRO was fated to be a toothless tiger, for public education and advocacy work would be neglected.

The Standing Committee of the National People's Congress in late January 1997 took action to annul in part or fully 25 of Hong Kong's ordinances (Note 1).   Most of them would not affect citizens' daily life.   But the partial annulment of the BRO, as well as the total annulment of the 1995 amended Public Order Ordinance (POO) and the 1992 amended Societies Ordinance (SO), would indeed adversely affect citizens' civil liberties (Note 2).

Sure enough, one of the first things SAR Chief Executive Tung Chee-hwa did was to start the process of emasculating Hong Kong's BRO, and drafting up a new POO and SO.   The proposals aimed to restore the licensing system whenever citizens wished to demonstrate or hold mass rallies, and to require registration whenever citizens desired to form a society.

Chief Executive Tung explained that the move was necessary because he had to strike a balance between civil liberties and social order.   The fact of the matter is, there is no inherent link between the two.   It is difficult to conceive that the more civil liberties individuals enjoy, the worse off, necessarily, the social order; or, reversely, that if we want to maintain social stability, we must limit citizens' basic rights. Hong Kong has in recent years become more liberal in terms of individual freedoms.   Yet this tendency has not been accompanied by a deterioration in social order.

The redrafting of both the POO and SO blatantly violates Articles 21 and 22 of the International Covenant on Social and Political Rights (Note 3).   These are citizens' fundamental rights.   Without them, freedom of speech would be difficult if not impossible.   If freedom of speech were stifled, the SAR government would be exposed to great danger, for the credibility of any government is built primarily on its willingness to deal with the truth, and let the truth be known.

Clearly, instead of going forward, the SAR government is leading Hong Kong on a course toward the repression and authoritarianism associated with the past. Many citizens in Hong Kong would say something along the lines of: never mind, we do not demonstrate, we do not associate with other like-minded people, so it is no big deal for the government to take away these rights from us.

But it would be a terrible mistake to think like that, for history teaches us otherwise. This was how Martin Niemoller, a well known German pastor, related his personal experiences: when the Nazis arrested the Jews, he did not protest, because he was not a Jew. When the Nazis harassed members of the communist party, he did not object, because he was not a communist. When the Nazis arrested the trade union leaders, he did not disapprove, because he did not participate in any trade union activities. Finally, when they dealt with him, nobody came to his rescue because all concerned people were gone.

If they are not checked, those in power and authority will always want to expand their power and influence. This is human nature.

Hong Kong's chief executive and provisional legislators are likely to legislate tough laws barring citizens from defaming or abusing the national as well as SAR flags and emblems. (The Hong Kong government had refrained from imposing any restriction against the abuse of either the Union Jack or the Five Star Flag in the colony.) They are also pondering what laws they should enact "to prohibit any act of treason, secession, sedition, subversion against the Central Government" (Article 23 of the Basic Law). Such changes threaten to restrict citizens' freedom of speech and expression. All in all, in post-handover Hong Kong the citizens are to enjoy a dramatically lower degree of civil liberty than they did in colonial days.

This is also true in the case of citizens' political rights. After a long struggle, appointments in the three-tier council system --the Legco, the two Municipal Councils and the 18 District Boards (DB)-- have been abandoned. Under the British, each citizen was eventually given the opportunity to elect his or her own DB member, urban or regional councillor, and Legco member on a one-person-one-vote basis

(Note 4).   In early May, however, Chief Executive Tung announced that he would re-introduce the appointment system in both the DB and the municipal councils.   The Preparatory Committee also decided to abandon the one-person-one-vote election system in the Legco, putting forth instead Chief Executive Tung's proposal to implement proportional representation (Note 5).   All these measures are aimed at not only cutting down the influence of the popular democrats, including the Democratic Party, but also cutting back the political rights of the masses.   In future, the business community will for certain regain the upper hand in the 3-tier council system.   All these measures are simply meant to reassure China.

In facing China and the powerful business tycoons and their lieutenants, Hong Kong citizens feel annoyed and helpless.   Yet, for the sake of Hong Kong, and the future of their children, they must break their silence and speak their minds.   They must do their best to preserve every safeguard for the basic rights in existence today, instead of giving each up one by one.

The Plight of the Poor

Hong Kong's economic success these past 30 years (1967-1997) has been phenomenal (Note 6).   The opening in May 1997 of the Tsing Ma Bridge, the world's longest suspension bridge, epitomized Hong Kong's tremendous achievements.   Hong Kong has created the world's busiest container port.   In 1996, it handled 13.2 million TEUs (Note 7).   According to the Airports Council International (ACI), Hong Kong's Kai Tak Airport has overtaken Japan's Narita and become the world's busiest airport, handling in 1996 more than 1.56 million metric tonnes of international air cargo, worth HK$160 billion. Hong Kong is expected to perform even better when the new Chep Lap Kok International Airport opens in 1998.

Especially in gauging the economic development of the past 10 years, Hong Kong has shown impressive trends.   Its total Gross Domestic Product (GDP) growth for the decade was 65% in real terms.

In 1996, Hong Kong was the world's 5th most important banking centre as well as foreign currency market, and the world's 7th largest stock market (in terms of its total volume and daily turnover). In terms of total exports, it became the 8th largest exporter in the world, with a total worth of HK$1,398 billion.

That same year, the Heritage Foundation (an American think tank) gave the territory thumbs-up in its findings, and declared that Hong Kong was the freest economy in the world for the second year in a row.

The World Economic Forum, based in Geneva, stated in its 1997 report that Hong Kong was the second most competitive region in the world, just after Singapore and ahead of the United States and New Zealand. That same year, *Fortune* magazine elected Hong Kong the most friendly region in which to do business.

Indeed, at least superficially, Hong Kong looks like it is a very modern and prosperous city. Millions of visitors come every year to enjoy the marks of its success (Note 8). Certainly, Hong Kong is a wealthy region. According to the February 7, 1997 issue of *Asia Week* (English-language edition), at the end of 1996 Hong Kong's GDP per capita (purchasing power parity) was US$23,200 (quite close to the Financial Secretary's 1996-1997 budget, which was HK$179,600). It has overtaken the world's two highly industrialized nations, Japan and Germany (US$22,200 and US$20,165 respectively); and is catching up to the world's highest, the USA (US$26,825) and Switzerland (US$25,070). It exceeded by far Canada (US$22,220) and Australia (US$19,960), the two countries to which most of Hong Kong's citizens have wanted to migrate; not to mention the past sovereign state, Britain (US$19,130) and the present one, China (US$2,935).

In reality, the wealth in Hong Kong is highly concentrated. According to the January 2, 1997 issue of *the Economic Journal,* on the last trading day of 1996 (December 31) the total volume of Hong Kong's stock market was slightly more than HK$3,515 billion. Yet ten families owned HK$1,638 billion (or 47%) worth of stocks (Note 9).

In his article, which appeared in the 1997 issue of *the Hong Kong Report* (published by the Hong Kong government), then Governor Chris Patten said that "the median incomes here have exceeded US$25,000 a head, but the majority of Hong Kong's citizens have not attained that level of comfort." This is definitely an understatement. The median monthly wage in 1996 was HK$9,500, yet more than 420,000 salaried people earned HK$4,750 or less per month.

The fact of the matter is that in Hong Kong the income disparity between those among the society's top 5% in terms of salary and the lowest 5% is a difference of 12.5 times; whilst in the neighbouring countries, Taiwan's ratio is 4.2:1, and Japan's only 4:1. In Hong Kong, in a government-subvented agency (such as a high school or social welfare agency) the administrator's salary is ten times that of a clerical assistant. The head of a university earns 20 times as much as a university janitor (not counting his fringe benefits, like housing, a chauffeured car, and the like).

According to government statistics, in 1986 the lowest 10% among the employed earned 1.6% of total salaries; this proportion dropped to 1.3% in 1991, and to only 1.1% in 1996. On the other hand, those among the 10% highest paid earned 35.5% of total salaries given in the territory. In this case the proportion increased to 37.3% in 1991, and to a staggering 41.8% in 1996. The gini-coefficient index also indicated that the rich and poor gap continued to widen: 0.373 in 1979, 0.476 in 1991, and 0.518 in 1996 (Note 10).

There has been little or no significant growth in salaries in real terms for low-incomed citizens in recent years. High inflation has been the major culprit. According to government statistics, in 1995 60% of the citizens earned HK$10,000 or less per month; 28% between HK$10,000 and HK$20,000; 10% between HK$20,000 and HK$50,000; and 2% more than HK$50,000 or above. As a result of Hong Kong's high cost of living, only 2% of its residents could be classified as rich, whilst 60% of the people live in relative poverty.

In the past 12 months, there have been five independent studies on Hong Kong's poverty problem (Note 11).   According to the one commissioned by Oxfam and Council of Social Service, 250,000 households in Hong Kong (or 640,000 individuals) live below the poverty line.   Each of these people has HK$7 or less to spend per meal (for 1997 adjusted to HK$8).   A university student tried to live on HK$26 per day for three days.   He went to bed hungry every night!

Despite the fact that about half the total population of Hong Kong has been provided with public housing, there are still tens of thousands forced to seek shelter under appalling conditions.   The government admitted that in 1996 there were still 165,000 people residing in temporary housing (including squatter huts), and 16,600 living on small junks (referred to as the floating population).   What was missing in government figures were the street sleepers, as well as the thousands who live in crowded private tenements.   The Society of Community Organization (SOCO) said that there are still 4,000 single men living in caged homes (Note 12).   Because of the high cost of housing (each square foot of apartment space is roughly HK$5,000, while rental is around HK$20 per square foot per month), even the quality of life of the middle class has been adversely affected (Note 13).

Hong Kong's treasury is one of the richest in the world.   The colonial government just transferred to the Special Administrative Region government a total of HK$700 billion: HK$154 billion from the accumulated surplus, HK$440 billion from the foreign exchange fund, and HK$25 billion from the land fund.   Despite the fact that the government possesses in its treasury this huge sum of money, its citizens are still waiting for the introduction of a comprehensive social security system whereby the retired, the sick, and the extremely poor would be taken care of and could live a dignified life.   Hong Kong is an international and modern city.   It is therefore disgraceful that it fails to meet the standard set forth in Article 9 of the International Covenant on Economic, Social and Cultural Rights which states:

"Everybody should enjoy the right to social security, including social insurance" (Note 14).

Public policies in Hong Kong in general do not favour the poor. On the contrary, they allow the rich and powerful to reap immense privileges and wealth in an extremely short period of time.   Twenty years ago, a group of concerned churchmen and academics pushed for the establishment of a central provident fund scheme.   It never materialized simply because the capitalists did not want to add 5% to their costs to contribute to the scheme.

The simple and low taxation system also greatly favours the rich. Right now the standard salaries tax in Hong Kong is 15%.   A young teacher who earns HK$20,000 pays 15% taxes; so does the highest salaried person (who earned HK$48 million in the financial year 1996-97).

Where does the responsibility for the formulation of public policies lie?   With the government, of course.   Yet this is only the obvious picture, as seen by the public.   In reality, by contrast, business tycoons have had the final word in every important public policy decision.   The high value land policy was the making of the property tycoons (all tycoons in Hong Kong are related to the property business one way or another).   The business tycoons are in full control of all public utilities, as well as the construction and operation of all super-structures in the territory.   Yet there is little or no public scrutiny.   Big businesses monopolize the property market, public transport, supermarket, retail food business, everything upon which the citizens' livelihood depends.

The business community has not only lobbied hard behind the scenes.   In a way, it has also controlled directly the government machinery.   The highest policy making body in the executive-led government in Hong Kong has been the Executive Council.   Up to the very last day of the colonial era, all ten non-civil servant members were appointed by the governor.   They were either business tycoons or closely related to the rich and the powerful in the community.

Before 1985, the Legco had the same arrangement.   Even ten years later, when all 60 members were directly or indirectly elected (Note 15), Legco, having the important task of monitoring the performance of the government, was still very much pro-business.

With the handover there has not been any improvement in the balance of power.   As a matter of fact, it seems to be tending toward an increasingly lopsided arrangement.   Chief Executive Tung was a business tycoon (Note 16).   His supporters and close advisors come from a similar background, while the members he has appointed to serve in the SAR's Executive Council have only symbolic grass-root representation.   Since the provisional legislature has excluded the democrats and the future legislature will limit their participation and role, the poor definitely will have an even weaker voice in Hong Kong's public policy decision-making process.

But most important of all, it is the Chinese government which favours this kind of arrangement: let the rich get what they want so that they will in turn contribute to Hong Kong's social stability and China's prosperity.   Undoubtedly, China and the rich tycoons who act on its behalf are less interested and committed to improving the well-being of the masses.   In fact, they have taken measures to curb the civil and political rights of the masses.   These measures will deprive them even further of what little voice they had during the colonial era.   It is important to note, however, that in the long run this kind of arrangement will hurt, rather than help, Hong Kong.   As Hong Kong continues to develop, it will require more participation from its citizens.   Yet these citizens will certainly hold back if their opinions are suppressed and their efforts ignored.   This explains why, in the long run, economic development means more than economic growth.   It requires a fairer distribution of wealth, as well.

Religious Freedom at Risk

Mainline denomination heads in Hong Kong, as represented by the chairman and the general secretary of the Hong Kong Christian

Council, have often told visiting dignitaries and journalists that the handover symbolizes "the birth of a new era" (Note 17).   They have also been quick to dispel worries about the fate of religious freedom, pointing to the guarantees in the Basic Law, especially Articles 32 and 141 (Note 18).   A few evangelical leaders, such as the former chairperson of the Hong Kong Chinese Christian Churches Union (HKCCU) (Note 19), have also tried to project a rosy picture to the rather pessimistic evangelical Christians.   Quoting Article 149 of the Basic Law, Rev. C. K. Liu promulgated that the religious policy, the Religious Affairs Bureau, and the Three-Self Church in China would not come to Hong Kong.   Rather, the Church in China and the Church in Hong Kong would be related to one another based on the principles of non-subordination, non-interference, and mutual respect.

This viewpoint put forth by leaders of the Church seems rather simplistic.   It is true that religious freedom is stipulated by law in the HKSAR, but how much a law can protect people is always subject to interpretation by the authorities, and is ultimately a matter of implementation by the law enforcement bodies.

Unfortunately, in a more authoritarian state those in positions of power not only make laws, they also implement and interpret these laws according to their personal likes and dislikes as well as interests. For example, the 1982 Chinese Constitution stipulates that "all citizens of China enjoy the freedom of speech, of the press, of assembly, of association, of procession and of demonstration" (Article 35).   But when the Chinese students in the spring of 1989 exercised those rights in Tiananmen Square, they were met with the People's Liberation Army's tanks and sub-machine guns.

For certain, when the ruling elite have considered their authority threatened or their course of action inconvenienced, they have resorted to anything possible to stop citizens from exercising their "lawful" freedoms, their rights.   The following incident illustrates this point vividly.

The Lutheran World Federation (LWF) had long ago decided that it was going to hold its ninth General Assembly in Hong Kong July 8-16, 1997.   This was recognized as a tremendous gesture on the part of the Lutherans to show their confidence in both Hong Kong and in China.   Preparatory work began in 1993.

In February 1996, however, the New China News Agency informed the LWF's local coordinating committee that since the LWF assembly was a matter straddling the handover on July 1, it had to be dealt with through diplomatic channels, i.e., the Sino-British Joint Liaison Group (JLG).   In the end, because of mounting pressure from the international community, China backed down.

The real reason why China objected was obvious.   It wanted undivided attention from the international media to cover the important event of the handover (Note 20).   The LWF's assembly taking place so near the handover would certainly steal part of the limelight.

In arguing its case, China was at least partially right in saying that this incident had nothing to do with the state taking away religious freedom from its people.   But this interference indicated that whatever practises were common in China could very well be carried over to Hong Kong.   In Hong Kong, international meetings --big and small, commercial, religious, and professional alike-- are held weekly if not daily.   Never before had anyone been required to ask permission from the colonial government.

The LWF incident has served as an important warning that the SAR government, acting on direct or indirect instructions from China, can step in and interfere in citizen's affairs at its whim (Note 21).   Citizens' freedom to assemble, demonstrate, associate, and speak are all vulnerable to restriction.   So, too, is the case with religious freedom.

Even if we take the Basic Law very seriously, trusting that it will be fully implemented in letter and spirit, the Basic Law only guarantees a "privatized faith." In other words, as long as citizens limit their religious practise to the confines of their temples, synagogues, mosques, and churches, or cooperate fully with the government in providing social services, they will have no problems. But when the faithful take their faith more seriously and apply it in the wider context, they may run into trouble with the authorities. For example, many Christians believe that since faith implies social concern, they must be concerned about issues such as human rights, democracy and social justice. If they take this course, sooner or later they will clash with the government and the powerful people in society. The Christian faith demands that Christians care for the weak and the young in society. When Christians come across people without food, it is natural that they give them some food to eat. The government authorities will also fully endorse this. Yet when they start asking about why poverty exists in an affluent society, they may run into trouble with the authorities.

The Chinese regime, and non-Christian leaders in Hong Kong as well, have always understand religious practise from a very narrow perspective. This narrow understanding of religion will certainly endanger Christians and the religious of any faith seeking to witness God's love and justice in the territory of the SAR.

Moreover, Article 23 has given the government a great deal of power to curb dissent and limit citizens' freedoms. It forbids citizens from engaging in "any act of treason, secession, sedition, subversion against the Central People's government," and in stealing state secrets. It also prohibits "foreign political organizations or bodies from conducting political activities in the SAR," as well as "political organizations or bodies of the region from establishing ties with foreign organizations or bodies."

This Article represents a black hole for the citizens of Hong Kong, especially those who want to exercise their freedoms. They could face dire consequences if the activities they conduct or words they utter cause embarrassment or displeasure to government leaders. Article 23 certainly hinders churches from maintaining a fraternal relationship with, for example, the Presbyterian Church in Taiwan, which advocates and supports the movement for an independent Taiwan. Likewise, Hong Kong's churches will be discouraged from associating with any American church which supports human rights in Tibet. The Roman Catholic Church in Hong Kong will eventually have to redefine its ties with the Vatican, unless the Vatican decides to sever its close ties with Taiwan. Religious freedom in this broader context will be curbed in Hong Kong sooner or later.

China is Hong Kong's sovereign government. In China, rule by powerful individuals is far more important than the rule of law, and the power of the rulers is far more important than individual freedoms. Now that the handover is behind us, no one of sound mind can believe that citizens' freedoms will remain in tact. China is not yet a signatory of the two important international rights instruments, namely the ICCPR and ICESCR. Deep down in their hearts, academics, journalists, professionals, and social activists in Hong Kong are not optimistic about the future of their freedoms. If freedom of the press, of speech, of assembly, of association, and of demonstration are curbed, we can hardly sit back and expect religious freedom to be immune to the danger of curtailment.

NOTES

1. The Standing Committee of the NPC annulled 16 Hong Kong laws in their entirety, and another 9 partially. A lot in the former category had something to do with the British colonial symbols and regulations. Patten's constitutional proposals were also entirely scrapped.

2. China explained that Britain should hand back Hong Kong in the state in which it existed when the Joint Declaration was signed in 1984. Anything which Britain had altered in Hong Kong unilaterally since 1984, China would reinstate in the pre-1984 form. But this arrangement is inappropriate. Hong Kong has developed by leaps and bounds in the past 13 years. New laws would have to be enacted while some of the old laws would have to be amended to cope with new situations. More than 1,000 pieces of new legislation have been introduced in Hong Kong since 1984. But China and the new SAR government have chosen to annul only the few which have had something to do either with elections or the liberalizing of restrictions on individual freedoms.

3. ICCPR Article 21 states that "the right of peaceful assembly shall be recognized," and Article 22 that "everyone shall have the right to freedom of association with others."

4. In the 1995 Legco elections, 30 seats were returned by the functional constituencies (in some functional constituencies, there were bloc votes by organizations or agencies; in others, individuals voted), 20 through geographical constituencies on a one-person-one-vote basis (direct elections), and 10 by DB members and municipal councillors.

5. In the proportional representation voting method, Hong Kong will be divided into five big constituencies. Voters have one vote only. Political parties will be allocated the number of seats

proportionate to the votes they received. For example, in the 1995 elections if such a method had been employed, since the Democratic Party got 50% of the votes cast, it would have been given 10 seats (out of a total of 20).   In reality, according to the single-seat single vote method in place at the time, the Democratic Party got 12 seats.

6.   Hong Kong started to evolve as a light industrial centre (manufacturing mainly textiles, garments and plastics) in the late 1950s. But Hong Kong's economic development as a centre of trade and finance in Asia began to take shape only after the riots in 1967.

7.   Please refer to Hong Kong's 1997-1998 budget entitled "Continuity in a Time of Change," paragraph 40.

8.   In 1996 alone, Hong Kong had more than 12 million visitors, about 3 million from mainland China and the rest from overseas, including Taiwan.

9.   Of these ten families, one was British (Swire), one Jewish (Kadoorie), one Malaysian Chinese (Robert Kuok), and one Chinese from the mainland (Yung). The other six were local Chinese business tycoons.

10.   Gini-coefficient index is an index measuring the rich and poor gap, from 0 to 1. Most of the developed nations have an index below 0.3.

11.   Five independent studies were commissioned: by Oxfam, Council of Social Service, Hong Kong Social Security Society, City University and Caritas.

12.   A caged home is an apartment filled with 3-tiered bunk beds. Many occupants build a fence around their bed's space, so it comes to look like there are a great many cages inside the

apartment.

13.   It has not been unusual to have one salary (say HK$12,000) of a
      young professional couple going directly towards the mortgage.

14.   Britain became a signatory nation of the ICESCR in 1976.

15.   In 1995, Legco became a fully-elected body, with 20 seats directly
      elected through geographical constituencies, 30 indirectly elected
      through functional constituencies (or professional groupings),
      and 10 by the election committee, constituted by all directly
      elected District Board members and municipal council members.

16.   Tung Chee-hwa resigned from the chairmanship of the Oriental
      Shipping Company when he declared his candidacy in
      September 1996.

17.   A quote taken from an interview by Kim Lawton of Religious
      News Service in the United States, April 1997.

18.   Article 32 of the Basic Law states: "Hong Kong residents shall
      have freedom of conscience.   Hong Kong residents shall have
      freedom of religious belief and freedom to preach and to conduct
      and participate in religious activities in public."   Article 141 says,
      "The Government of the HKSAR shall not restrict the freedom of
      religious belief, interfere in the internal affairs of religious
      organizations or restrict religious activities which do not
      contravene the laws of the Region.   Religious organizations shall,
      in accordance with law, enjoy the rights to acquire, use, dispose
      of and inherit property and the right to receive financial
      assistance.   Their previous property rights and interests shall be
      maintained and protected.   Religious organizations may,
      according to their previous practise, continue to run seminaries
      and other schools, hospitals and welfare institutions and to
      provide other social services.   Religious organizations and
      believers in the HKSAR may maintain and develop their relations

with religious organizations and believers elsewhere."

19. HKCCCU was founded in 1915.   Unlike HKCC (founded in 1954), whose membership is denominational and ecumenical (with such organizations as the Hong Kong Bible Society, YMCA, and the YWCA), HKCCCU's membership consists of Chinese congregations only.

20. It is widely believed that between 6,000 and 8,000 journalists from all over the world were in Hong Kong in June and July to cover the event of the changeover of sovereignty as well as to record the general mood of local citizens.

21. Church leaders themselves can be highly impressionable.   In July of 1997, when the LWF sought to draft a statement expressing concern about human rights conditions the world over, an intended reference to China led to the abandonment of a bold project.   Concerned that any mention of China would cause it offense, local Lutherans succeeded in convincing the Assembly participants that the mild reference be dropped.   Such obvious oversight of a major human rights offender could only be concealed if the entire project were aborted.

6

Disintegration of the Social Fabric

Vested Interest of the Wealthy

In traditional Chinese society, government officials were highly regarded. As members of the educated strata they ranked just below the ruling elite, and above farmers and manual labourers. Traders occupied the bottom of the social ladder. People looked upon traders with disdain because they were considered selfish, always looking solely after their own interests.

Indeed, traders are fundamentally profit-oriented. Many of them do not even care about what products they are selling. A case in point from Hong Kong's history would be the East India Company, later branching out to become Jardine, Matheson and Company. In the 1800s it was responsible for selling tonnes of opium to the Chinese.

As early as the 1820s the British government already had the intention of establishing a colony in Hong Kong. Its aim was not to transmigrate its people to Hong Kong, as it had done in Australia and New Zealand.   Neither did it aim, as it had done in India, to get natural resources, for Hong Kong had none.   Its sole aim was to create a stepping stone and a supply base for the British traders who wanted to trade in China.

In order to run their operations, the British traders employed a great many coolies from China (Note 1).   These labourers were treated like slaves, invariably exploited.   Their pay was meager, and they were often beaten by their masters.

As Hong Kong today looks back over the past century and a half, it is faced with the difficulty of finding any traders in its history who possessed a clear conscience.   In fact, Hong Kong --as an entrepot until the 1950s, as a light industrial centre in the 1960s and 1970s, and, finally, as a financial centre since the 1980s-- has been run basically according to the wishes of business tycoons.   They have controlled everything, from economic and social policies, down to the livelihood of the masses.   In fact, they are the culprits responsible for making Hong Kong a highly unjust society, with the wealthy enjoying immense privileges and the poor struggling merely to survive. Business ethics have been foreign to the Hong Kong businessmen and businesswomen.   When land and labour costs became expensive, these pragmatists moved their manufacturing plants elsewhere, mostly across the border into mainland China.   In 1984, the labour force in the manufacturing sector amounted to 1.1 million workers. Nowadays, only 385,000 people are working in factories located within Hong Kong.   Many aging factory workers have lamented that they were loyal to their bosses, but their bosses failed to reciprocate.   Many middle aged women who worked in factories for 20 or 30 years (the best part of their working lives) are now unemployed because their factories moved away from Hong Kong.

Business tycoons in Hong Kong are no longer only interested in making money (they have already made plenty).   Their main objective now is to expand their market share in order to acquire enough power so as to control and dictate the market.   Take the supermarket business and real estate market as two examples.

Six months ago, "Welcome" and "Park 'N Shop," two leading supermarket chains, engaged in a price war for two weeks.   They offered a 10% discount on all the items on store shelves.   Naturally, they did not make any money on many of the items.   But at the end of the day, many smaller retail stores were forced out of business.   As a result of this price war, the market share for these two chain stores increased from 75% to almost 80%.

Despite the huge property market, there are actually just four developers which have exercised control over 75% of the market.   The four are: Cheung Kong, Sun Hung Kai, Henderson Land, and New World.   These big property developers seldom talk about the number of apartments or buildings they own.   Rather, they tend to talk about the acres of land in their reserves.   To retain control over scarce resources represents leverage and influence.   Consequently, they still aim to buy more and more land in the territory.

An important issue for Hong Kong, supposedly the world's freest economic zone, is "monopolization."   In Hong Kong, public utilities, public transport, and tunnels (Note 2) are all franchised, rather than administered by the state.   Ownership by large companies negates the benefits which come from competition in a free market, so that these "public services" are essentially "monopolized."   The general public has no say in their pricing.   Likewise, in the case of banking in Hong Kong, the lending rate is unusually high where one would expect competition among banks to benefit the consumer.   In fact, the lending rate is usually 4% higher than the interest people receive from their savings accounts.   This is because the major banks in Hong Kong get together and form an association similar to that of a cartel.   Representatives meet often and they agree upon the interest rate and the prime lending rate.

It is true that Hong Kong has adopted a laissez-faire (least-intervention) policy. Rules and regulations are kept to a minimal. Those people with courage and luck can always gain an upper hand. Yet rules and regulations are by no means unimportant. It is because of legislated requirements that business tycoons spend lots of time trying to befriend senior government officials who are responsible for formulating public policies, rules and regulations (Note 3). The governor, who was responsible for appointing members to sit on the Executive Council (the highest policy making body in Hong Kong) and the Legislative Council (until 1985, when 24 out of 56 Legco members were indirectly returned by professional groups and districts), certainly gave due consideration to the recommendations made by business tycoons. As a matter of fact, even up to this day, the business community is in full control of both the Legco and Exco.

But as British rule was to end in 1997, the far-sighted local business tycoons all fixed their attention on China. Since they had no record of being "patriotic Chinese" they had to catch up. Many of them, such as one business tycoon who donated the building costs for a university in Amoy, started to give big donations to China. They have also been investing heavily in China (Note 4). To Chinese leaders such gestures have been deeply appreciated. Many business tycoons have through such avenues succeeded in becoming their good friends.

Another strategy business tycoons in Hong Kong employ to bolster their own prospects is to manipulate public opinion so that whatever they themselves think becomes the mainstream perspective in Hong Kong.

For instance, business tycoons have convinced China that the goal for Hong Kong must be the maintainence of its "stability and prosperity." In order to achieve social stability, a limit must be set on individual freedoms. Therefore, Hong Kong's citizens need to make sacrifices in terms of their personal rights. Furthermore, they argue that as China takes over Hong Kong, there has been no marked drop in citizens' confidence levels regarding the future. Directing the public's attention, they point to several "positive" trends. The crime rate has gone down in the past year. The stock market is booming. The Hang Seng Index has soared from 13,000 to 15,000 points. The Tsing Ma Bridge has just successfully opened. The new airport in Chep Lap Kok, arguably the world's most modern and advanced, will start to operate in mid-1998. Indeed, the rich and the powerful have not only painted a rosy picture for Hong Kong's future, but they have tried their best to make sure that this picture becomes the dominant view both locally and overseas. In order to propagate this view, they have launched the "Better Hong Kong Foundation." The Foundation has employed one of the public relations industry's top people, Ji Man Fung, to be its chief executive. Reportedly the budget for the foundation is a staggering HK$100 million. This in addition to the HK$100 million spent for the extravaganza to mark the return of Hong Kong to China on June 30 and July 1, 1997. For sure, those who have not agreed with their view or those who have tried to sabotage their propaganda have been met with suppression. It should not be surprising that Tung Chee-hwa condemned Martin Lee and accused him of bad-mouthing Hong Kong, despite the fact that all Martin Lee did was to communicate to the international community (including the US President and the Canadian Prime Minister) a few worries which Hong Kong's citizens would face after the handover.

Generally, the rich and the powerful are extremely self-interested. But this tendency is especially pronounced in Hong Kong. There they are removed from the masses. They know very little how the poor live. A former secretary of health and welfare was invited to visit a caged home. She was shocked by what she saw. The chairperson of an influential charity organization in Hong Kong was alerted that the conditions of some of the premises which her organization managed were appalling. In the beginning, she categorically denied such situations ever existed; but when the residents urged her to come and stay for a night, she promised she would look into the case!

Hong Kong has become a much less caring community now compared with that of 20 years ago, despite the fact that much of its population experienced hardships before securing a good life.   A major reason is because the rich and the powerful have become extremely self-centred.   Even if they have been engaged in charitable work, it has been because "good publicity" helps their business endeavours.   The rich and the powerful have set a rather poor example for the people of Hong Kong.

Cooptation of the Elites

As a British Crown Colony secured through the trade-inspired Opium War, Hong Kong started out as a money-oriented, polarized society.   It was made up of but two categories of people: the rulers and the ruled.   The British ruling class enjoyed enormous power and many privileges.   The Chinese, over whom this rule was exercised, were treated as decidedly different, in some cases even physically segregated (Note 5).

As time went on, Hong Kong became more prosperous and complex.   The British decided to absorb a few Chinese who were well educated and fluent in the English language to help them rule Hong Kong.   Li Shing and Ho Kai in the early years, and Robert Ho Tung and Chau Shauson in the pre-war years, were some of the most famous ones on whom the British relied so heavily.   As a matter of fact, the British throughout their rule in Hong Kong spent a great deal of effort intentionally cultivating a class of local elites.   As a rule these elites were intelligent, well-trained, disciplined and fiercely loyal to their masters.

The Chinese who migrated to Hong Kong were extremely hard-working.   They were prepared to ride through many storms and make all the neccessary adjustments in their lives.   On the positive side, these Chinese immigrants were able to adapt to the changing conditions in the territory, such as the influx of refugees in 1949 and 1950 (Note 6), the total embargo on China imposed by the United

Nations through a special resolution in 1951 (Note 7), the riots in 1956 and again in 1967, the oil crisis in 1973, the collapse of the property market in 1981, and the slump of its stock market in 1987.   The bad side of this tenacity was that these Chinese immigrants had no principles.   They did not consider Hong Kong to be their home. They came to Hong Kong to earn money.   They would work for any people who could give them more money.   Injustices and social ills were of no concern to them.   That explained why the wealthy and the powerful in Hong Kong could so easily get away with anything.

Despite this apparent bravado, Hong Kong's citizens are very afraid to offend those in authority.   The colonial setting, the Chinese culture of honouring the elderly, and the citizens' concern for self-gain are the major contributing factors.   Now that the handover is past, this will become even worse.   Generally, Hong Kong's citizens are much more afraid of China than of Britain.   China is now one of the most powerful nations in the world.   Its regime is controlled tightly by the Chinese Communist Party.   It lacks any internal mechanism that functions to check and balance power.   Fearing any possible heavy-handedness, Hong Kong's citizens, especially the elites, have learned to adjust their thinking and to self-censor their words and deeds.

In June, the Hong Kong Alliance in Support of the Patriotic and Democratic Movement in China (the Alliance) wanted to erect in a garden a bronze sculpture entitled the "Pillar of Shame" (Note 8). During the debate at the Urban Council (which manages all parks and gardens in the urban area), the most outspoken councillor who objected the move by the Alliance was reminded that eight years ago it was he who suggested the "Goddess of Democracy" be erected to commemorate the crackdown of the democratic movement in Tainanmen Square.   His reply was extremely simple: "The times have changed" (Note 9).

The powerful elites in Hong Kong, cultivated by the British, have basically turned to Beijing.   One could say that the British did a rather poor job.   They did not train these elites to be independent.   Rather, these people were only trained to be obedient and to rely on the "source of power" (before 1995, it was London; after 1995, it became China).   Indeed, today everybody wants to get close to Beijing, especially Hong Kong's business tycoons and elites.   Nowadays a position or title given by China --such as Hong Kong affairs advisor, Hong Kong district affairs advisor, Preparatory Committee member, Selection Committee member-- is worth much more than any knighthood or medal given by the Queen (Note 10).

In order to get close to the source of power, business tycoons in the territory generally do two things.   Many offer contributions (donate a school or invest in a project in China), or advice (meaning literally words pleasing to the ears of Chinese leaders; some of these words are related to how to rule Hong Kong).   In addition, they make sure the people over whom they have influence do not speak ill of China.   What results is self-censorship.

Self-censorship is a very serious problem in Hong Kong.   Hong Kong's development relies heavily on press freedom and academic freedom.   Now we seldom see a leading academic in the territory speaking his or her mind.   Scores of them have been absorbed by China as its advisors on Hong Kong affairs, or to serve in the Preparatory Committee.   Heads of all six universities in Hong Kong are members of China's appointed Preparatory Committee.

Press self-censorship poses an even more serious dilemma.   In early May 1997, the Department of Journalism and Communication of the Chinese University of Hong Kong released the results of a study regarding the attitude of the local journalists.   According to that finding, half of the respondents (Note 11) said they would be very careful in their critical reporting of China.   More than a third said that they would be cautious in criticizing the business community.   One in five admitted practising self-censorship.   The study also indicated that 5% of the local journalists believed that in order to preserve stability, the press should refrain from exposing the darker side of the society. Furthermore, 11% said that for the overall welfare of the community, the press should give up some of its freedom. Finally, more than 50% believed that with the handover press self-censorship would be even worse.

What has encouraged self-censorship? In the case of the media, responsibility for self-censorship lies largely with China. China has always wanted the media to be the regime's mouthpiece. Within China, journalists must report only what the regime expects of them. In order to make sure Hong Kong's journalists fall in line, China has refused "unfriendly journalists" permission on several occasions to enter the mainland and cover important events (Note 12). Xi Yang, a Hong Kong reporter, was jailed 12 years for "unauthorized reporting."

Newspaper owners have also contributed to the mood of self-censorship. Two leading newspapers, *the South China Morning Post (SCMP)* and *Ming Pao*, have been bought by Malaysian businessmen Robert Kuok and Zhang Xuerxing. Both have tremendous trade interests on the Chinese mainland. It is far too much to expect them to allow their newspapers to be seriously critical either of China or of Hong Kong's business tycoons. In early 1997, *the Asian Wall Street Journal (AWSJ)* accused *Ming Pao* of self-censorship, a charge which *Ming Pao* vehemently denied. To those who have been reading the daily for a decade or two, they would most likely agree with the comments made by *AWSJ*. Months before the handover, *SCMP* appointed the first publisher of the English-language *China Daily* to be an "advisor"!

There is no doubt that free access to information and press freedom go hand in hand. Without a free flow of information, there can hardly be press freedom. Without press freedom, the whole society will certainly be worse off. Hong Kong is a free society. Its free economy depends heavily on a free flow of information and in turn a free press. If media people continue to practice self-censorship, Hong Kong will soon become a less competitive business centre and a more closed society.

Acquiescence of the Masses

Members of the business community have been trying their best to broadcast a sense of optimism about China and about Hong Kong's future.   But deep down in their hearts, they do not really share this kind of optimism.   If they were in fact optimistic about the future of China and Hong Kong, why have they obtained foreign passports? Why have they moved their registered offices away from Hong Kong? Why have they decided to diversify their investments despite the fact that Hong Kong is still the best place in the world in which to make money?

Like the members of the business community, local elites and the middle class have indicated that they are not confident about Hong Kong's future.   Between 1982 and 1989, 150,000 permanent residents emigrated the territory, heading mostly to Canada, Australia and the United States.   After the Tianamen crackdown in June 1989, between 30,000 and 60,000 permanent residents left Hong Kong each year (Note 13).   Because of a lack of job opportunities overseas, many who secured citizenship abroad have since returned.   According to one count, as many as 600,000 Hong Kong permanent residents are now holding an overseas passport.   Other than the 180,000 British passport holders (Note 14), the rest have had to go away physically for three to five years.   To some this has meant an uprooting of their entire families.   To many others it has meant establishing "split families," where the husband works in Hong Kong while the rest of the family lives overseas.   If these people have so much confidence in Hong Kong's future, why would they have to resort to such drastic measures?

There is no doubt that Hong Kong is suffering from an unprecedented crisis of confidence.   Little of this has been reflected in recent surveys, for people just don't want to talk about it.

As mentioned previously, of the 6.3 million people now living in Hong Kong, 45% fled China after 1949.   In addition, 30% are their descendants born in Hong Kong. How can these refugees and their descendants have confidence in the regime they tried to escape? All of them know what it means to live under a totalitarian regime. For the older generation, they went through endless political movements in China in the 1950s. For the middle aged, they witnessed the 10-year Cultural Revolution. For the younger generation, they have witnessed the People's Liberation Amy (PLA) opening fire on the people they were supposed to protect!

Of course, one can argue that these extremely dehumanizing acts by the Chinese regime represent events in history particular to a certain time. China has changed a lot in the past eight years. Yet, as long as China maintains its one party rule system, the Chinese leaders will remain intolerant of dissent and criticism. Under such circumstances there cannot be a truly free and open society in China.

Still haunted by their past experiences in the mainland and having no way to leave for another country, come what may, most of the citizens have to deal with life in post-handover Hong Kong. In order to survive, they remain silent and take whatever is given to them.

With pressure to adopt an acquiescent mindset, the majority of Hong Kong's citizens have become even more withdrawn. On the whole, people have become increasingly indifferent. An "everybody for themselves" attitude has been spreading like a contagion. Hong Kong's affluence and material comfort are obvious. What is absent is the caring spirit in the community. Domestic workers and imported labourers (Note 15) have often been exploited and maltreated, illegal children uncared for, Vietnamese refugees discriminated against. Increasingly, there are more and more cases of child abuse and family violence reported.

To conclude, one can say that the community leaders in Hong Kong have set bad examples. They no longer want to distinguish between what is right and wrong, what is good and bad, as well as what is responsible and irresponsible. In order to promote their influence and benefits, all they do is court those who are in higher positions and trample on those who are below them. This is an extremely unhealthy social atmosphere. Consequently, people in Hong Kong are today forced to live as less-than-dignified human beings.

If all these negative trends should continue, sooner or later, the society of Hong Kong will disintegrate.

NOTES

1. "Coolie" is a derogatory term referring mainly to transport labourers.

2. There are five mountain tunnels and three cross harbour tunnels in the territory. They all charge tolls which serve to earn a profit for the corporations that own them.

3. Business tycoons routinely made contributions to the Conservative Party in the United Kingdom. Tung Chee-hwa admitted that he himself had donated HK$500,000 when the party was in power.

4. Even two noted British firms tried to sell a significant part of their shares to Chinese enterprises.

5. Chinese, for instance, were not allowed to live on Victoria Peak, where most of the British resided.

6. According to government records, as many as one million refugees from mainland China fled to Hong Kong between 1948 and 1953.

7. China entered the Korean War in 1950, on the side of North Korea. To punish China, the United Nations forbade its members from trading with China. Trade between the United States and China, for example, came to a complete halt. Hong Kong's entrepot functions were jeopardized as a result of this action by the UN.

8. The "Pillar of Shame" is a 7-metre, dark copper sculpture by Danish artist Jens Galschiot Christophersen. Its form is made up of a score of painfully twisted human bodies.

9. The meaning of the saying is clear. Eight years ago, the British

were still in charge.   They could act as a buffer warding off any incursion into Hong Kong by the People's Liberation Army.   But now, China is in full command.   Hong Kong's citizens should behave themselves and not offend China.

10.   The British had a nice way of rewarding Hong Kong citizens for their loyalty and distinguished public service.   Twice a year (the New Year and the Queen's birthday), hundreds were honoured and awarded the C.B.E. (Commander of the British Empire), O.B.E. (officer), M.B.E. (member), or B.M. (Badge of Honour). The highest honours used to be the knighthood.   But in 1993, Lydia Dunn was given a life peerage.   She became a baroness.

11.   900 questionnaires were sent to 22 local news organizations, including both the print and the electronic media.   553 were returned.

12.   After June 4, 1989, guidelines known as the "seven clauses" were given to all local journalists.   They must apply for a permit to go to China to cover any event.

13.   For a number of years after June 4, 1989, Canada received more of these immigrants than any other country, taking in about 24,000 Hong Kong residents per year.

14.   About 50,000 households in Hong Kong were given British passports by the British Nationality Scheme, introduced in 1991 to keep key personnel in Hong Kong.

15.   There are about 130,000 Filipinas working in Hong Kong as domestic helpers.   In addition, thousands of imported labourers are employed to work on the new airport projects, various highway projects, as well as the strategic sewage disposal system.

PART THREE

TOWARDS A CITIZENS' CHURCH

The Church of Hong Kong, like the society it seeks to serve, is itself at a crossroads. Its past contains evidence of change as well as continuity. It must now decide whether, in light of the changes arising from the handover, it will turn and address the new needs which are in evidence, or continue along the well-worn path. Clearly, there is little choice in the matter if the Church is to be true to its mission. But perhaps the requirements of shifting onto a new course are not yet obvious to some. Three logistical factors must first be addressed: Who does the Church represent? What is the best method to employ in serving these people? What is the message it seeks to convey in order that these people may be served? The Church is here on earth to serve the little ones --those whom Jesus Christ singled out for his special attention some 2,000 years ago. In order to combat the tendencies to disempower the masses, the Church must lead the way in speaking out. Finally, the message it should trumpet is that of personal sacrifice for the good of all. The Church must learn again how to preach the gospel of sacrifice. In so doing, it will be leading by example.

7

A Church for Others

The Church Renews, Ever Renewing

"The Church renews, ever renewing" ("ecclesia reformata semper reformanda") is the motto of the Presbyterian Church of the United States. Indeed, the Church needs constant self-examination and renewal. "Renewal," as this author often argues, is an essential feature of the Church of Jesus Christ. Renewal reflects our humility in acknowledging that this world is in constant flux, and our need to respond to these changes appropriately. Yet there are certain conservative tendencies, and the Church is also prone to them, becoming either entrenched in the worldly, or, equally problematic, disengaged from it. Renewal ensures that the Church moves self-consciously, leading the world to be more just, participatory, and sustainable --eventually, the kingdom of God on earth.

The Christian Church, since its inception almost 2,000 years ago, has recognized the need to overhaul from time to time. For example, in the first three centuries, many church councils took place so as to enable leaders to clarify the meaning of the Christian Faith. But in this effort to improve, the simple incarnate word (the word became flesh) was made complicated. Creed after creed was shrouded by fancy terms and deep meanings. Consequently, rather than equipped to strive for a "living faith," believers were left to follow precepts many of which they could not themselves comprehend.

In medieval times (5th century to 15th century AD), the Church in the West was very much institutionalized. Its management of land, property and people led it to become a solidly built system of its own. Its heirarchy (including the pope and bishops) even ruled a few principalities in Europe, expressing bluntly the organizational power of the Church.

Then, in the early 16th century, came the Protestant Reformation, the first in a series of successive attempts at renewal. The reformers opposed the "imperial church," so over-organized and so close in its relationship to state power. But, with their attempts at simplifying, Protestant leaders such as Martin Luther, John Calvin, and Huldreich Zwingli made the Christian faith an intellectual exercise for the well educated. Pietism and the missionary movement in the 19th century represented a shift in focus: directing Christianity at and appealing to the ordinary people, especially people with no Christian background in the Old World, the New World, Asia and Africa. But these efforts drew people's attention toward the spiritual and supernatural world, to the exclusion of the secular, the everyday realm of actual existence. Finally, the Ecumenical Movement of the 20th century represents a reaction to the main streams of the Christian Church in the previous century. It advocates that the Church should engage actively in the world, and that Christians should be taught to take their life circumstances seriously, while seeing how they fit into larger issues.

Looking at the Church in Hong Kong, though only 150 years old, it has also gone through several rounds of transformation. It has attempted in its own way to respond to new needs in a changing Hong

Kong. In the beginning, it attempted to give educational opportunities to the local youngsters. When in the 1950s the refugees from mainland China were in need of relief and welfare, the Church responded. In the 1960s, when children needed schooling, the Church built hundreds of schools (Note 1). And in the 1970s, when all kinds of social and human needs became imminent as a result of the socio-economic transformation in Hong Kong, the Church introduced social work methods developed in the West to meet those needs.

But after 40 years of rapid growth, the Church in Hong Kong has become a victim of its own success. It has become far too institutionalized, and has consequently lost its dynamic force to respond to needs arising from the political changes in Hong Kong brought about by the 1997 handover. It has developed a dependency syndrome, having always to rely on the financial support of the government and the rich. It is no longer able to transcend the many conflicts the territory faces with regard to its return to China. Its full collaboration with the establishment in running schools, social centres, clinics, and hospitals has caused it to lose its independence and autonomy. Incapable of voicing criticism itself, it fails to educate its students in critical and independent thinking. Responsible for managing the bulk of social services in Hong Kong, it refuses to cross the threshold and enter the realm of social reform.

The Church in Hong Kong has built itself a mammoth empire. Its preoccupation now is with survival if not continuous expansion. Church leaders have to spend lots of time to manage this huge Church enterprise, so much so that they often complain they see no meaning in all this. The Church provides and expands on all these services just for the sake of acting --never asking itself why or for whom it acts. Perhaps the answer is something to be avoided. Indeed, what these services do is extremely beneficial for the Church, enhancing both its image and influence. In a word, the Church has grown self-centred.

Now is the time for the Church in Hong Kong to renew itself. It must turn inside out. Rather than be self-serving, it should aim to genuinely serve the world.   The Church is for the world.

The Christian Church, though inaugurated at Pentecost (c.f. Chapter 2 of *The Acts of Apostles*), actually began when Jesus left his disciples at his Ascension.   *The Synoptics* (the Gospels according to *Mark, Matthew* and *Luke*) all end with Jesus's final commandment:

> Go out to the whole world; Proclaim the good news to all creation.
> > (*Mark* 16:15, *Jerusalem Bible*)

> Go, therefore, make disciples of all the nations; baptize them in the name of the Father, the Son and the Holy Spirit.
> > (*Matthew* 28:19, ibid.)

> And that, in his (Christ's) name, repentance for the forgiveness of sins would be preached to all the nations, beginning from Jerusalem.
> > (*Luke* 24:47, ibid.)

It is strikingly apparent that in *the Synoptics* Jesus's commandment to his disciples and to the early church was to "go out into the world" rather than to stay inside the church building or within the confines of the warm fellowship.   It is equally clear that the locus --the activities or mission-- of the church ought to be conducted in the entire world.   "The world is the church's parish," so says John Wesley, the founder of the Methodist Church both in the United Kingdom and the United States.   All the nations and all the people in the world constitute potential beneficiaries of the Church, those for whom the Church exists to serve.

In fact, the whole New Testament reflects this world view, this open-mindedness of the early Church.   For example, in the Johannine writings, especially in the fourth Gospel (the Gospel according to *John*), the message "God so loved the world" (*John* 3:16) depicts one of the two major themes of the whole gospel. God's love and the whole world (the **oikoumene**) are inseparable and total (Note 2). God's love is for every inhabitant of this earth. Therefore, the ministry of the Church must be extended to all. This type of universalism is also very much alive in the Pauline Letters. According to Paul, God's righteousness and God's salvation are for all, since God was responsible for all creation, and since every human is a sinner requiring God's mercy.

There is little doubt that, in general, the inclusiveness and universality of the Church has been depleted, even corrupted. Owing to human greed and insecurity, the Church has become a rather self-serving club. Most of the things it does fail to contribute positively to the push towards creating an increasingly open and humane society. It obviously needs to be reformed. One of the first things the Church should come to terms with is that the Church is in the world and that it is for the world.

The "Mission" of the Church

The majority of Christians in Hong Kong consider their church to be either a place for fellowship, or a place where they can refocus their lives and enhance their spiritual growth, mainly through worship on Sundays. This conceptualization of the Church is, of course, far from adequate.

Regarding the nature of the Church, the Old Testament gives us ample insights. Chapter 12 of *Genesis* marks the beginning of a people who became conscious of its identity and calling. Abram (later known as Abraham) was called upon by God with the following words:

I will make you a great nation;
I will bless you and make your name so
famous that it will be used as a blessing.
I will bless those who bless you

I will curse those who slight you
All the tribes of the earth
shall bless themselves by you.

(*Genesis* 12:2-3, *Jerusalem Bible*)

God blesses the people God chooses; makes them "great" and "famous." But being Christian is not only about receiving. The people whom God chooses and blesses should use whatever is bestowed upon them by God to be a "blessing" to "all the tribes" (Note 3). Here, "all the tribes" refers to everyone inhabiting the earth.

The message in *Genesis* 12 also illustrates this point: God's blessings will be bestowed upon the Church. Simultaneously, God demands that the Church use these blessings not for its own gain, but to benefit the world. It is against God's will that Christians or the Church should keep God's blessings only for themselves.

Nowadays, most Christians joining the Church are motivated by selfish purposes, rather than the will to build a healthier, a better society. Many worship and pray fervently, hoping that God will bless them and their families. They become the receptacles rather than channels of God's blessings.

The classical prophets in the Old Testament (Note 2) consistently picked up this theme and expanded on it very elaborately. Let us look at the four servant songs in *II Isaiah* (Note 4). God gives all anointed servants (the Church) a mission which is in this world. Oftentimes it involves witnessing, such as helping those in immediate need. But other times it is about expressing concretely God's love in order to achieve a long term and common good --social justice.

Here is my servant whom I uphold,
my chosen one in whom my soul delights.
I have endowed him with my spirit
that he may bring true justice to the nation.
He does not cry out or shout aloud,

or make his voice heard in the streets.
He does not break the crushed reed,
nor quench the wavering flame.
Faithfully he brings true justice;
he will neither waver, nor be crushed
until true justice is established on earth,
for the islands are awaiting his law.

(Isaiah 42:1-4, *Jerusalem Bible)*

It is not enough for you to be my servant,
to restore the tribes of Jacob
and bring back the survivors of Israel;
I will make you the light of the nations
so that my salvation may reach to the ends of the earth.

(Isaiah 49:6, ibid.)

The Lord Yahweh has given me
a disciple's tongue.
So that I may know how to reply to the wearied
he provides me with speech.
Each morning he wakes me to hear,
to listen like a disciple.
The Lord Yahweh has opened my ear.

(Isaiah 50:4, ibid.)

See, my servant will prosper,
he shall be lifted up, exalted, rise to great heights.
As the crowds were appalled on seeing him--
so disfigured did he look that he seemed no longer human
--so will the crowds be astonished at him,
and kings stand speechless before him;
for they shall see something never told
and witness something never heard before.

(Isaiah 52:13-15, ibid.)

The Old Testament writings (Note 5) rarely talk about the

mission of the Church directly.   Yet where there are elaborations on God's care for humanity, as well as on human responsibility, there are many allusions to such mission.   Let us look at the final hymn of praise in *Psalms* (Note 6).   In this hymn (*Psalm* 141-150), God is praised because,

> Yahweh, forever faithful,
> gives justice to those denied it,
> gives food to the hungry,
> gives liberty to prisoners.
> Yahweh restores sight to the blind,
> Yahweh straightens the bent,
> Yahweh protects the stranger,
> he keeps the orphan and widow.
>
> (*Psalms* 146:7-8, ibid.)

If God cares for these "little" people, would God not expect the Church to care for them as well?

This, then, is the message of the Old Testament (Note 7).   God demands that the chosen, the Church, care for God's whole creation, especially the individuals who are in need.   Indeed, this is the way we should read God's purpose for human beings in both creation stories (Note 8).   In the first narrative, we read, "Be masters of the fish of the sea, the birds in heaven and all living animals on earth" (*Genesis* 1:28 b).   In the sense of having God's image (*Genesis* 1:26), as masters and mistresses, human beings certainly have a responsibility to care for God's creations, rather than to deplete them according to their own wishes.

What does all this mean for the Church in Hong Kong?

Worship is essential to the life of the Church; but it must be extended beyond all church buildings.   To worship God is to glorify God, to magnify God's Holy Name.   Therefore the Church cannot turn a blind eye on exploitation, repression, hunger, and mass genocide no matter where on earth such attrocities occur.   These injustices and offences bring God's name into disrepute. To glorify God both in the sanctuary and in the world are two sides of the same coin. Christians in Hong Kong must recognize this fundamental relationship and seek ways to extend their worship life beyond the church edifice.

Likewise, Christian fellowships should not be inward looking. They must be extended to the entire world so that every community in the world can become a caring community.

Christians who join the Church should realize that they are there not for self-gain. On the contrary, they should be prepared to make sacrifices so that more people in this world can enjoy a fuller life (c.f. *John* 10:10).

Care for the Weak and the Young

God created the whole world. As the Ash Wednesday collect (a short prayer) of the Episcopal Church states so vividly, "God hates nothing that he has made." In fact, every page of the Bible affirms that God is love. So great is this love that God gave the world God's only son (*John* 3:16). But although God loves the entire human race, special care is extended to those little ones, for they are particularly needy. *The Synoptics* underscore this point when they depict the life and ministry of the Incarnate Jesus.

Let us first look at *Matthew*. The Gospel mainly consists of five teaching blocks: Chapters 5-7 (On Discipleship); Chapter 10 (On the Mission of the Disciples); Chapter 13 (On the Kingdom of God); Chapter 18 (On Pastology) and Chapters 24-25 (On the Last Judgment). Jesus's teachings are "missional." The first teaching block (Chapters 5-7) pertains to the conditions or the ethics of his followers. It begins by stating that his disciples should be the "light of the world" (5:14) or the "salt of the earth" (5:13). It ends by elucidating their carefree lifestyle (6:19-34). The second teaching block (Chapter 10) is about how his disciples are "sent." The words sending and mission go together.   In fact the origin of the word "mission," or "missio," means "sent."   A person who is sent is always a person who has a mission. In the third teaching block (Chapter 13), "the parables of the Kingdom" are actually Jesus's teachings about God's Kingdom and Church.   The Church is responsible for helping bring forth God's Kingdom into this world.   The fourth teaching block (Chapter 18) is about Jesus's command to his disciples, that they should pay special attention to care for the weak and the young.   In the first part of this teaching block (18:1-20), Jesus carefully elevates the status of the little ones or the weak ones.   Jesus goes so far as to say that the Kingdom of God actually belongs to them.   His disciples should therefore pay special attention to these who are often overlooked.

In the last teaching block (Chapters 24-25), Jesus goes a step further by fully identifying with the little ones.   This is what Jesus said, "I tell you solemnly, in so far as you did this to one of the least of these brothers (and sisters) of mine, you did it to me" (25:40).   To put it another way, the Church should stand alongside the weak and the young in the same manner as Jesus who fully identified himself with the hungry, the thirsty, the foreign, the naked, the sick, the imprisoned.

The Gospel of *Luke* is clearly a gospel for the poor.   This is how *Luke* recorded the beginning of Jesus's ministry (Note 9).

> The spirit of the Lord has been given to me,
> for he has anointed me.
> He has sent me to bring the good news to the poor,
> to proclaim liberty to captives and to the blind new sight,
> to set the downtrodden free,
> to proclaim the Lord's year of favour.
>
> (*Luke* 4:18-19, ibid.)

Like the Prophet Isaiah, Jesus intended to bring the "good news" to the poor.   The poor are the captives, the blind and the downtrodden.   To put this into the contemporary context, Jesus cares not only for those who are materially poor, but also for those oppressed and exploited, or those who have lost a sense of meaning in their lives.

Luke 4:18-19 is what the entire Gospel of *Luke* is really all about. The rest of the chapters merely substantiate how Jesus put his goal into practice. In *Luke*, we come to realize how Jesus cared for the poor. According to *Luke*, the poor are those marginalized as well as those looked down upon by society. As a matter of fact, in the whole gospel, Luke narrated very vividly how Jesus especially cared for four groups of people: women, Gentiles, sinners and those who are lost, as well as the materially poor.

Women. In the middle East, in both the Jewish and the Palestinian worlds, women had no social status. In *Numbers*, we read about an early census of the Israelites. They counted only the adult males (*Numbers* 1:2), not women or children. Even in the New Testament times, the Apostle Paul admonished the women faithful to cover their heads when going to prayers and worship (*I Corinthians* 11:2-12). The message is very clear: women were treated as non-persons. But contrary to the mainstream customs and traditions of their time, Jesus and Luke gave special attention to women. In chapter one, for instance, the main characters are not men, but, rather, two women: Elizabeth, the mother of John the Baptist, and Mary, Jesus's mother.

Jesus, as depicted by Luke, regarded women highly. On the Sabbath, Jesus violated an important Jewish law by healing not a man, but a woman (13:10-17). Jesus appreciated greatly certain qualities women possessed. For example, women's persistence (the women and the lost drachma in 15:8-10; the importunate widow in 18:1-8); the great humility of a woman sinner in 7:36-50; and, above all, the examples of service to people and to God (the story of Mary and Martha in 10:38-42).

Gentiles. On the whole, the Jews were a narrow-minded and fairly exclusive people. In Biblical times, they viewed themselves as

God's chosen people.   Non-Jews were "unclean" and ought to be excluded from their society.   That explains why James and John (two of Jesus's closest disciples) suggested when the Samaritans refused to receive Jesus and his disciples in a village in Samaria that Jesus "call down fire from heaven to burn them up" (9:55).

But Jesus did not share their sentiment.   Moreover, he regarded highly the Samaritans.   In the "parable of the Good Samaritan," the person who assisted the Jewish merchant who fell into the hands of robbers was not the priest who saw what had happened, nor the Levite who passed by, but a Samaritan.   This Samaritan, considered an arch enemy by the Jews, put his business aside and responded to a Jew who needed help.   Jesus promptly told the Jewish lawyer who came for advice about what he should do, "Go, and do the same yourself" (10:37).   In the midst of all the learned rabbis and priests in the Jewish community, Jesus put forth as an example of service to others a person whom they despised.

Furthermore, in the healing story of ten lepers (17:11-21), only one returned and gave thanks to Jesus.   He was not a Jew, but a Samaritan.   Even one who did not follow the Jewish traditions and customs knew how to be thankful.   How much more should the devout Jews?   It was most ironic that Jesus asked his proud and self-deceiving Jewish compatriots to follow the examples set forth by the people whom they looked down upon, namely women and Samaritans.

Sinners and the Lost.   One of the liveliest chapters in Luke is Chapter 15.   The whole chapter consists of three parables depicting God's mercy: the lost sheep (15:4-7), the lost coin (15:8-10), and the lost sons (or the prodigal son and the dutiful son) (15:11-31).   Jesus's special attention to sinners and the lost is consistent with an earlier claim by Jesus, "I have not come to call the virtuous, but sinners to repentance" (5:32).   Jesus accepted totally those whom people rejected in his day, among them tax-collectors.   He went to be a house guest of Zacchaeus (19:1-10) (Note 10).   He forgave the sinner who was nailed to the cross beside him (23:39-43). Last of all, Jesus lifted up the prayer of a publican and criticized that of a "self-righteous Pharisee" (18:9-14), for the Pharisee had exalted himself while the tax-collector had humbled himself and prayed for God's mercy.

The Poor. The poor have, throughout history and throughout the world, been looked down upon by others. But this is not so in *Luke*. In the Magnificat (or Mary's Song of Praise) (1:46-55), these words are included:

> He has pulled down princes from their thrones
> and exalted the lowly.
> The hungry he has filled with good things,
> the rich sent away empty.   (1:52-53)

Jesus looked upon the poor especially as the people for whom he should care. This was what he uttered in the very beginning of his ministry at Nazareth, "He has sent me to bring the good news to the poor..." (1:18 quoting from *Isaiah* 61:1). Later in his teaching, Jesus admonished those who wanted to give dinners or lunches in his honor to, instead, invite the poor, the crippled, the lame and the blind (14:12-13). Lazarus, a poor man, was comforted in the last judgment, while an unnamed rich man who was not kind to Lazarus was sent to hell (16:19-31). While Jesus did not directly condemn people who were rich, nevertheless he specifically warned against the danger of hoarding possessions (12:13-21) and of the lack of trust in Providence among the wealthy (12:22-32).

The Church in Hong Kong needs to take this long discussion very seriously. It needs to be reminded of the danger of becoming self-serving, that it should be more mindful of those in need. The Church in Hong Kong must cease to depend on and side with the rich and the powerful. Like Jesus, it must stand alongside the marginalized, the socially deprived, and the exploited. Taking this stance will be the beginning of a new Church in Hong Kong, a Church which cares, a Church which is truthful to God's calling.

NOTES

1. The Hong Kong Council of the Church of Christ in China, the third largest school sponsoring body in Hong Kong, ran only four primary schools in 1962.   In 1982, it managed 64 schools directly.

2. The two themes put forth in *John* are: "God is love," as set out in Chapter 3 of the Gospel, and "God is spirit," set out in Chapter 4.

3. In the original text, or in the Revised Standard Version (RSV) of the Bible, the words "all nations" are used.

4. *II Isaiah* denotes Chapters 40-55 of *Isaiah*.   The four servant songs are: 42:1-4; 49:1-6; 50:4-9 and 52:13-53:12.

5. The Old Testament Writings consist of:
    Poetry: *Job, Psalms* and *Proverbs*.
    Historical Literature: *Ezra-Nehemiah, I* and *II Chronicles*.
    Prophecy: *Daniel*
    The Five Scrolls: *Song of Solomon* (read at Passover), *Ruth* (read at Pentecost), *the Lamentations* (read at the remembrance day of the Fall of Jerusalem, AB), *Ecclesiastes* (read at the feast of the tabernacles) and *Esther* (read at Purim).

6. The 150 psalms are divided into five parts, viz. 1-41, 42-72, 73-89, 90-106, 107-150, each ending with a doxology or hymn of praise. Many O.T. scholars consider that the entire 150th psalm is a doxology.   But this author would like to argue that actually Psalms 146-150 can be considered an extended doxology.

7. Basically, the Old Testament consists of the "Law" (*Genesis, Exodus, Leviticus, Numbers* and *Deuteronomy*), the "Prophets" (Former Prophets - *Joshua, Judges, I* and *II Sammul, I* and *II Kings*; Latter Prophets - *Isaiah, Jeremiah, Ezekiel* and twelve minor prophets), and "Writings." *Jeremiah* 18:18 and *Luke* 24:44 make similar allusions.

8. There are two creation stories in *Genesis*, namely 1:1-2:4a (from the "P" source) and 2:4b-25 (from the "J" source).

9. It is a quote from *Isaiah* 61:1-2.

10. In the Eastern cultures, to share a meal is a gesture of acceptance; to be a house guest therefore bears deeper meanings still.

8

An Alternative Voice

A Responsible Church

The Church is in the world and exists for the world. In its service to the world, it responds to the needs of the world.

In the past 150 years, the Church in Hong Kong did in a way try to respond to contemporary realities. When the young needed education, the sick needed hospital care, and the elderly needed institutional care, the Church responded by building schools, hospitals and homes for the aged. After World War II, and especially following the 1949 change in government in the mainland which brought about an economic transformation in Hong Kong, the Church in Hong Kong responded by providing not only much needed relief to hundreds of thousands of refugees, but also school places for their children. After the riots in 1967, when Hong Kong undertook a social transformation, the Church introduced many social work-related services to help solve some of the human as well as social problems. One criticism often levelled against the Church in Hong Kong is that it did not go far enough. It consistently neglected to solve the more deeply rooted problems, problems related to the structure of the whole socio-economic and political system. In facing imminent changes connected with the handover, the Church remains an onlooker.

Since the 1985 ratification of the Sino-British Joint Declaration regarding the future of Hong Kong, a political transformation has been underway in the territory. One of the most urgent needs to reveal itself has been for **preparation**. Firstly, Hong Kong's citizens require preparation in order to enter comfortably and confidently a new era, one in which Hong Kong is partly, but not completely, integrated politically with China. Secondly, they require preparation in order to take care of their own affairs, thus fulfilling the promise made by China about "Hong Kong people ruling Hong Kong." If preparation is so clearly necessary, and people and institutions are gearing themselves toward new circumstances, why, then, is the Church not preparing itself and the people it serves for new things to come? Why is the Church in Hong Kong not prepared?

As already mentioned, from its inception as a Crown Colony in 1843 the society of Hong Kong was divided in two. The rulers were the British merchants and the officials of the colonial administration. The ruled were the Chinese who came from the mainland. But as Hong Kong became an increasingly important and vital entrepot, the British rulers had to rely more and more on the local elites to administer it. The Church was consequently invited as a "partner" to provide all types of social services to the wider community. Thus it came to be that by serving those in need, the Church served the government and the wealthy --those who constituted the ruling class. Eventually, institutional churches (their leaders especially) themselves became a part of the ruling class. It is not surprising, therefore, to find that in the last 30 years the Church in Hong Kong has been fairly happy to help the rulers maintain the status quo.

Contrary to the general perception, the handover does not mean radical changes in the territory as far as the basic social structure is concerned.   There will still be the ruling class and the ruled.   The only change involved is the identity of the sovereign power.   After the handover, China will replace Britain.   Several years ago Hong Kong business people already began shifting their reliance away from the British colonial administration which had looked after their commercial interests.   As a matter of fact, in the last days of the colonial administration, only a handful of the most senior civil servants remained loyal to the British flag (despite everyone having taken an oath of loyalty).   Most of the senior officials moved between both the colonial government and the SAR government, rationalizing that the civil service in Hong Kong was politically neutral.

Nevertheless, there will be many radical changes to the political system with the handover.   The basic premise of the Hong Kong Special Administrative Region of China represents monumental change: with the exception of defense and foreign affairs, the SAR government is ultimately responsible for running Hong Kong.   As a territory of China it is now endowed with a high degree of autonomy and is administered by local citizens.

Since China is not going to send a governor to rule Hong Kong, Hong Kong can, in principle, for the first time in its history choose its own chief executive and legislative representatives.   Concerned people, particularly the Church, ought to stand up and make sure that such arrangements are not limited to words on paper, but are realized in actual practice.

But institutional Church leaders have, on the contrary, adopted a permissive stance: since China is Hong Kong's sovereign power, China can do whatever it pleases in the territory.   Such a position is defended with the reasoning that because China can gain a lot by treating Hong Kong kindly, there is no apparent cause for concern (Note 1).

Moreover, the same Church leaders often argue, there is no way

Hong Kong can confront China. Geographically, China is 10,000 times bigger than Hong Kong. As far as the population is concerned, Hong Kong's 6.3 million is dwarfed by China's 1.255 billion. China is the world's most powerful regime, with the world's largest army and the world's best organized public security bureau. Its leaders are very much intolerant of dissenting voices, and have used their might to silence and suppress.

Certainly, the establishment in Hong Kong has been trying hard to sell a framework of living to its citizens: by all means keep your horse racing, your gambling (Note 2), and your night life (Note 3), but do not attempt to challenge the authorities. A set of cartoons in the Milwaukee Sentinel, an American newspaper, represented the Chinese government's ideal, and the likely result of its pressures: a Hong Kong once mobilized will fall silent; the crowds of past demonstrations will give way to vast, empty spaces come the handover!

The rulers in Hong Kong are using their extremely powerful propaganda machine to mold local public opinion, emphasizing that Hong Kong is an economic, not a political, city and society. Capitalism has worked well in Hong Kong in the last 40 years. It has brought economic miracles to Hong Kong. Therefore it must be preserved at all costs.

Indeed capitalism works for people in Hong Kong; but it works for only a small group of capitalists or entrepreneurs. For the majority, they work hard but their benefits are limited to the crumbs which fall from the table. That explains the huge gap between rich and poor in Hong Kong. The motto "Stability and Prosperity" (uttered repeatedly by senior Chinese leaders in reference to the future of Hong Kong, and echoed by the local business community) is actually fairly repressive. It discourages the have-nots from speaking up, encouraging them only to work hard within a highly lop-sided system. Continuing to instill a slave mind-set among the masses, it robs them of their basic human dignity.

If Church leaders find it difficult to speak up, it is then up to concerned Christians to do so, as they are an equally vital part of the Church.   Silence means endorsement, and the Church simply cannot remain silent in this critical period of time.   If the Church as a community should remain silent now, while there is still space to maneuver, what will be its future?   Three or four years after the handover, when silence has allowed a gradual narrowing of space for dialogue and participation, the Church will find it even harder to speak up and perform its functions.

Dare to Speak Up

Speaking up does not necessarily mean confrontation.   Yet, even if the authorities perceive speaking up as confrontational, people must continue to speak up.   Speaking up is the only way Hong Kong can continue its phenomenal growth and development.   Speaking up means exercising reason.   It means creating space for people to think and imagine without inhibitions.   Most important of all, it means dispelling the habit of telling lies.   In a word, speaking up offers an alternative voice.   Oftentimes this alternative voice may be a counter voice to the voice of the powerful.   In being a critical voice it may cause embarrassment to the powerful.   But in the long run, alternative voices can keep those in power honest and thus more responsible in whatever they do.

Tung Chee-hwa, HKSAR's Chief Executive, decided long ago that public dissent needed to be curbed.   He therefore instructed his administration to rewrite the Public Order Ordinance and the Societies Ordinance.   During the latter years of the colonial rule, Hong Kong's citizens could demonstrate whenever they liked.   If there were more than 50 people, they had to inform the police (mainly so that traffic could be directed and managed).   But after the handover, police must issue prospective demonstration and rally organizers a "notice of no objection" to their planned events.   (Tung insists such formal notification of approval does not constitute a permit.   But whatever you call it, it is a fact that organizers of mass public gatherings are required to apply to the police to secure full consent.) Before the handover, citizens could freely form an association; after the handover, an official permit is required.

In issuing a consultation document entitled "Civil Liberties and Social Order," Tung argued, on the one hand, that he did not intend to take away any civil liberties now enjoyed by Hong Kong's citizens. But at the same time, he argued that there must be a balance between individual freedoms and the social order. Surprisingly, the majority of citizens in Hong Kong buys Tung's ideas. Yet, not only do the new ordinances contravene both Hong Kong's Bill of Rights and the ICCPR (Articles 21 and 22), they also raise important questions about Hong Kong's current and future systems. As responsible citizens, we must ask why a new Societies Ordinance and a new Public Order Ordinance are necessary. Did Hong Kong become any worse off as far as social order was concerned following the amendment of the Societies Ordinance in 1992, or the amendment of the Public Order Ordinance in 1995? Whose decision was it to make more changes now, and how was this decision reached?

In reality, what is at stake is the fact that because of the enactment of these ordinances, the powerful become even more powerful and the masses become even more powerless. For a healthy society and polity, Hong Kong needs alternative voices to counter the viewpoints of a limited few.

In order to please China, Tung Chee-hwa has repeatedly said that the people in Hong Kong must look towards the future. To do that, Tung has suggested, local citizens must forget the past which includes the commemoration of the June 4, 1989 crackdown on the pro-democracy movement in Beijing. But the fact of the matter is Tung has never asked the Chinese leaders to settle with the past. As long as Chinese leaders refuse to re-evaluate what happened on June 4 and its aftermath, it will be impossible for the people to separate the current Chinese regime from the one which used force to suppress the peaceful demonstrations of its own citizens.

Undoubtedly, it is difficult to say things which are not pleasing to the ears of those in authority.   But there is no alternative for the Church.   The Church must speak up if it is to be true to its calling. God called the prophets in the Old Testament to be God's spokesmen and spokeswomen.   Nowadays, God calls members of the Church who are faithful to God to speak up.   God's servants should not be afraid to speak up, even if it means confronting the powers and principalities directly.   This is a major characteristic of the prophets in the Old Testament, and should be emulated.   They dared to stand up and speak out against the powerful, especially those who abused their powers.

A classic example of this resolve is evidenced in Elijah's denunciation of Ahab, King of Israel, 874-853 BC (Note 4).

Ahab had wanted to acquire the vineyard belonging to Naboth which was near his palace in Jezebel.   But Naboth would not sell.   So Ahab's queen, Jezebel, instigated a trial based on a fabricated charge for which Naboth was eventually sentenced to death.   After the execution of Naboth, Ahab took possession of the vineyard.   Elijah criticized Ahab and branded him a murderer and robber, and foretold the doom of the royal house (*I Kings* 21:1-24).

Likewise, the Prophet Amos was not afraid to speak the truth as he saw it.   Highly critical of the wealthy business people who dominated the Israelite society in the eighth century BC, he voiced these scathing words:

> Listen to this, you who trample on the needy and try to suppress the poor people of the country, you who say, "When will New Moon be over so that we can sell our corn, and Sabbath, so that we can market our wheat?   Then by lowering the bushel, raising the shekel, by swindling and tampering with the scales, we can buy up the poor of money, and the needy for a pair of sandals, and get a price even for the sweepings of the wheat."   Yahweh swears it

by the pride of Jacob, "Never will I forget a single thing
you have done." Is this not the reason for the
earthquakes, for this inhabitants all mourning, and all of it
heaving, like the Nile, then subsiding, like the river of
Egypt?

(*Amos* 8:4-8, *Jerusalem Bible*)

Jesus, who came as the Prophet in New Testament times, went a
great deal further than the classical prophets in the Old Testament in
confronting the powerful who used their God-given advantages to
suppress the masses. At least this was the impression given in the
earliest Gospel, *Mark*, likely to have been completed in the late 60s AD.

Basically, *Mark* is made up of 15 controversial stories (Note 5).
These stories are divided into two categories. Some stories illustrate
how Jesus's actions violated the Jewish law, traditions or customs.
These include, for example, how Jesus healed a paralytic (2:1-12),
befriended the sinner and tax collector (2:13-17), worked on the
Sabbath (2:23-3:5), and ate with unclean hands (7:1-13). There are also
stories relating to the questions or tests put forth to Jesus by the
Pharisees, the scribes, the priests. These include whether Jews should
pay taxes, (12:13-17) the question of resurrection (12:18-27), Jesus's
position on divorce (10:2-9), and which of the ten was the greatest
commandment (12:28-34).

All this would not have happened if Jesus had not come, or if he
had spoken and acted in full accordance with Jewish law and custom.
If that had been the case, Jewish religious leaders would have
continued to rule with rigid regulations perhaps even until this day.
But Jesus came. Moreover, he confronted the religious leaders who
used their authority as upholders of the law to suppress the Jews and
rob them of their human dignity.

One of the commandments which the Jews continue to follow
faithfully is the fourth commandment: keep the Sabbath holy (Note
6). To celebrate Sabbath essentially is an affirmation of God's hand in

creating everything on earth and in the heavens (Note 7). Since God worked for six days and rested on the seventh, so should all human beings. After a period of work, all people need "refreshment." Keeping Sabbath was required by Jewish law as a means of protecting common workers, of making sure they had at least one rest day per week. But what about those who had no food? Should they work on the Sabbath in order to feed themselves, or observe the Sabbath? This was the dilemma Jesus's disciples faced. They themselves were busy assisting in Jesus's ministry, and often ended up going hungry as a result of missed meals. So it was not surprising when one day, while passing through a cornfield, they decided to pick ears of corn to eat. The Pharisees saw what happened and filed a complaint to Jesus that his disciples had broken the Sabbath law (2:23-28).

Later that same day, when Jesus went into a synagogue in the city, he healed a person with a withered hand. The Pharisees protested even louder (3:1-5).

Jesus went about his work on the Sabbath, and endorsed what his disciples did, because to Jesus, "Sabbath was made for man, not men for the Sabbath." In other words, rules and regulations, though important, are made for the protection and well-being of the people.

According to Mark, Jesus confronted the priests, the scribes, and the Pharisees about the way they used rules and regulations to control people. Naturally they were extremely annoyed. They considered Jesus to be rocking the boat. Such a perception explains why early in Jesus's ministry "the Pharisees went out and at once began to plot with the Herodians against him, discussing how to destroy him" (Mark 3:6, Jerusalem Bible). The rulers in the Jewish community could not tolerate the undermining of their authority.

China comes to Hong Kong with power and might (Note 8). Pro-China politicians and community leaders who serve as its agents or proxies in Hong Kong have in their words and deeds demonstrated this vividly. For example, Simon Li Fook Sean, a deputy chairman of the Preparatory Committee, warned Hong Kong's citizens that neither China nor he would like to see demonstrations taking place once every three days, and mass rallies once every five days. Hong Kong's citizens have clearly been intimidated by such statements, and show signs of refraining from speaking their minds. In order to combat this political censorship, the Church must speak up. In speaking its mind, the Church can also encourage many others to be less afraid of voicing their opinions.

In the beginning, it may be somewhat difficult for the Church to communicate its genuine concerns about those in authority. For, in general, and in all likelihood, speaking up will be considered confrontational, even subversive. But the Church, like those it is meant to serve, must overcome its fears.

Truth Telling

What China really needs is someone who dares to speak the truth, someone like the Church. China follows strictly the one-party rule, with authority concentrated in the executive. Thus it lacks the mechanisms for assessment and accountability competition brings to an otherwise stable political system. In other words, the Chinese Communist Party is not enriched by voices other than its own. Since it misses objectivity and criticism from outside, its overall development, and that of the state it administers, is rather slow and limited.

The economic development of a country is also dependent in large part on accurate information and critical assessment. Myanmar (Burma) was a rice exporting country before the 1960s. But after becoming a highly repressive military regime, its economy was ruined. It was forced to become a rice-importing country. Likewise, the living standards in Hong Kong and the Philippines were about the same in the early 1960s. But after Ferdinand Marcos came to power and introduced authoritarian rule for some 14 years, the Philippine's GDP per capita dropped behind Hong Kong's to a level 1/9 that of the its former equal (Note 9).   The same case could be made of European countries, particularly Germany.   The living standard in Eastern Europe became significantly lower than that of Western Europe only after experiencing rule by totalitarian, communist regimes.   When East and West Germany reunited in 1990, it was found that the economy in East Germany had been practically bankrupt under its former system.

As ordinary people throughout the world are too afraid to speak up against those in authority, the Church, because it cares, must discharge its social responsibility by being a social conscience, by speaking up.   But first the Church must maintain a distance from those in authority, namely the government and business tycoons.

As we have seen in Hong Kong and in China, the rulers consistently co-opt young and bright intellectuals, as well as leaders who are representatives of certain sectors in the community, to help them rule the territory.   Once these people are absorbed, sooner or later they become junior partners to the rulers.   They enjoy more influence and privileges.   In return, they have to serve the rulers by defending whatever the rulers do.   It is too much to expect that once they are co-opted they can maintain their independence and work from within.

The Hong Kong Christian Council (HKCC) and many of its members decided to participate in the Selection Committee. Participation was considered by all sides as a gesture of goodwill to China.   When challenged, the HKCC et al. argued that the Selection Committee had legal basis.   According to the Basic Law, it would help China select the first SAR chief executive.   But as the Provisional Legislature has no legal basis, they said that they would not take part in the election of the 60 Provisional Legislative Council members. (Anyway, the Basic Law requires the Selection Committee to do one job only, viz. the selection of a CE).   But at the end of the day, Simon Sit (the chairman of the HKCC), Fr. Luke Tsui, and Bishop Peter Kwong each took part in the election of council members as well, a responsibility apparently required by the Chinese authorities.

As a prophet, another role for the Church is to remind people that there is always another side which they need to consider seriously. The Israelites were in need of a god or an idol on which to focus their attention when they were out in the desert. So they made a golden calf. But Moses risked the wrath of the majority and pointed out that this golden calf could only give them a false sense of security (c.f. Exodus 32:1-35). Likewise, when the Prophet Hosea realized that the Israelites, though continuing to worship God, had in reality turned away from God in their hearts, he had the courage to issue the following message:

> This is why I have torn them to pieces by the prophets, why I strengthened them with the words from my mouth, since what I want is love, not sacrifice; knowledge of God, not holocaust.
>
> (*Hosea* 6:5-6, *Jerusalem Bible*)

And when he saw the highly unjust society which existed in the pietistic Israelite community, the Prophet Amos did not hold back his condemnation:

> I hate and despise your feasts, I take no pleasure in your solemn festivals. When you offer me holocausts, I reject your oblations, and refuse to look at your sacrifices of fattened cattle. Let me have no more of the din of your chanting, no more of your strumming on harps. But let justice flow like water, and integrity like an unfailing stream.
>
> (*Amos* 5:21-24, ibid.)

Today, when everybody in Hong Kong is so engrossed in the pursuit of making money, the Church needs especially to remind people that they do not "live by bread alone" (Note 10).

The message is even more pertinent to the rich in Hong Kong, so preoccupied with getting nearer to the source of power just so that their wallets may become fatter. In order to do that, they are quite prepared to say things which they themselves may not believe.

Sir S.Y. Chung, a former senior executive councillor under colonial rule, defended the recent reintroduction by the SAR government of the appointment system in municipal councils and district boards, saying that it served to balance the interests of different parties. "This is not a retrogression of democracy, but a step forward," responded Chung to suggestions that the new government was appointing sympathizers in order to reduce the influence of contending voices (ref. to June 19 issue of *SCMP*, p.19 and editorial).

Those in authority always want to justify their decisions. Many of their rationalizations are simply white lies. Therefore, it is even more vital that the Church should speak the truth, speak that which it really believes.

One time, this author presented a paper at an international conference sponsored by the University of San Francisco. After his presentation, a scholar from Malaysia came up to him and said that he was deeply touched by the presentation. He elaborated a bit by saying that the other scholars had spoken from their heads, while this author had spoken from his heart.

To speak from the heart means to speak without speciousness or false pretense. It means, instead, to speak with honesty.

The Church should speak from its heart.

For over a century and a half, youngsters in Hong Kong have been taught to be obedient and well-behaved. Following the example of others, they concentrate on working hard, climbing the social ladder, and making lots of money. They have been shaped into beings possessing only tunnel vision. They have never been trained to ask questions nor encouraged to engage in independent thinking.

As a start, this is an important area where the Church should concentrate. It should enable young people to acquire an analytical mind and not follow blindly what others think and say. When China condemned Chris Patten for his constitutional reform proposals, the Church should have set an example and examined on what grounds were China's actions justified. China insisted that since the 1995 elections were not conducted according to its plan, China must dismantle the 3-tiered council system in Hong Kong, hence the setting up of the Provisional Legislature is justified. The Church should ask whether all this is consistent with the Joint Declaration and the Basic Law. China also insisted the 1995 amended Public Order Ordinance and the 1992 amended Societies Ordinance be restored in the original form, because Britain should give Hong Kong back to China in the same conditions as 1984. The Church must enable the people to ask why: with more than 1,000 pieces of new laws enacted or amended after 1984, why did China pick on only these very few?

There is no doubt that the future of Hong Kong lies in what China does with respect to Hong Kong, as well as what changes take place within the mainland, including the evolution of the Chinese Communist Party. Therefore, China needs to be reminded of what is at stake should Hong Kong not be doing well. But equally important is the fact that Hong Kong's future depends on its citizens, whether they care and dare to express their concern. The Church can assist in this whole process of being a prophetic and catalytic agent.

NOTES

1. China is the number one investor in Hong Kong, the source of more than HK$3,300 billion.   China also earns a good portion of foreign exchange via Hong Kong (up to a-third of its foreign exchange annually).   So certainly China will not kill Hong Kong. Moreover, Hong Kong is to be made an example for Taiwan's return to China.   If Hong Kong should go down the drain, it will deter Taiwan from rejoining China.

2. Horse racing in Hong Kong is one of the biggest enterprises.   In the 1996-97 season, excluding off-course betting, the total bets amounted to HK$92.3 billion (HK$12.3 billion were taxes).

3. A senior Chinese official used to put the hearts of Hong Kong's citizens at rest by saying, "after the handover, horse racing will continue and so will dances in dance halls."

4. Elijah was a prophet of the ninth century BC from Tishbe of Gilead in the Northern Kingdom.

5. The 15 controversial stories are:

    i.   Cure of a paralytic - the Son of Man has authority on earth to forgive sins (2:1-12)
    ii.   The call of Levi and Eating with sinners - I did not come to call the virtuous, but sinners (2:13-17)
    iii. On fasting - Jesus brought forth a new era (2:18-22)
    iv.   Work on Sabbath - Jesus was the master even of the Sabbath (2:23-3:5)
    v.   Allegations of the scribes - the source of power for Jesus (3:22-30)
    vi.   The traditions of the Pharisees - these made God's words null (7:1-13)
    vii. The Pharisees ask for a sign from heaven - the meaning of signs (8:11-13)

viii.   The question about Elijah - the pioneer has come (9:9-13)
ix.   The question about divorce - the rule of God is superior to the law of Moses (10:2-9)
x.   The authority of Jesus is questioned (11:27-33)
xi.   On tribute to Caesar - first test on Jesus (12:13-17)
xii.   The question of resurrection - a second test on Jesus (12:18-27)
xiii.   Which is the greatest commandment - third test on Jesus (12:28-34)
xiv.   Jesus condemned the hypocrisy of the scribes (12:38-40).

6.   This is the fourth of the Ten Commandments, "Remember the Sabbath day and keep it holy" (*Exodus* 20:8).

7.   God created the world in six days and he rested on the seventh (*Genesis* 2:2-3).

8.   The deputy commander of the PLA stationed in Hong Kong hinted in mid-June that the immigration and customs officers in Hong Kong should exempt him from regular procedures and checks whenever he crosses the border.

9.   According to a recent issue of *Asia Week*, the Philippines' GDP per capita (purchasing power parity) was US$2,660; this compared to Hong Kong's US$25,000, as reported in *The Hong Kong Annual Report: 1997.*

10.   This is a direct quote from *Deuteronomy* 8:3.   The Israelites were reminded that even in their most difficult days in the wilderness, Yahweh fed them and saved them from starving to death.   There is much more than food that people should be concerned about.

9

The Gospel of Renunciation

Redefining "Evangelism"

In the past 40 years, mainline church leaders have concentrated on the development and management of buildings and programmes. Meanwhile, congregations oriented toward "evangelism" have concentrated on leading more people into their "fold" or "fellowship" (Note 1). These latter churches often encourage their members to devote time periodically to help distribute leaflets on street corners and in letter boxes, or to do home visits in the evenings or during the weekends. The purpose is to invite people to come to their special church gatherings or Sunday services. These congregations also support financially or provide volunteers for a great many Christian organizations whose specialty it is to do evangelism in schools, hospitals, universities, or to target street sleepers, factory workers, or night workers. Reportedly there are about 200 such para-church organizations in Hong Kong.

In the past two decades, these evangelical congregations have also been busily involved in planting new congregations. Peace Gospel Centre had only four congregations by the end of 1977. Fifteen years later, there were 20. The Wanchai Church of the Church of Christ in China had two congregation 20 years ago. Now it has eight. Christian evangelical organizations and evangelical congregations often send missionaries overseas and sponsor short "gospel" tours in China. Members are often encouraged to go. All these efforts pay handsome dividends. Their churches grow rapidly; the general atmosphere of these churches by and large is extremely lively.

Very few Christians either within or outside the evangelical churches dare to criticize all these evangelistic efforts. To neglect to preach the gospel would be considered practically sinful.

But the "evangel" or "gospel" which the churches in Hong Kong preach needs to be looked at carefully. Generally, it points out that all people are sinners. In order to be saved, they must believe in Jesus. But what does it mean by believing in Jesus? The answers given by the evangelists are often vague, moralistic and extremely simplistic.

The gospel which the early Church preached is quite different. There is only one theme in the apostolic preaching (Note 2). It is not only about the death of Jesus. But more importantly it is about his resurrection. Hence the core of the gospel is "But God raised him (Jesus) from the dead" (*Acts* 13:30; c.f. *Acts* 2:24; 3:15; 4:10; 5:30 and 10:40). Jesus died. God resurrected him. These are two key components of the Christian Gospel. Unfortunately, Christians oftentimes are taught the second part, i.e., if they believe in Jesus, they have a new life, a life full of possibilities. What the whole Christian Gospel asserts is that in order to bring in a resurrected life, Jesus must die first. In other words, grace is never cheap. It can only be brought about by self-sacrifice. Indeed, this is how Jesus called his disciples: "If anyone wants to be a follower of mine, let him renounce himself and take up the cross and follow me" (*Mark* 8:34, c.f. *Matthew*

10:38; 16:24 and *Luke* 9:23 and 14:27).   Dietrich Bonhoeffer (1906-1945), one of the most influential thinkers and theologians of this century, put it very simply: Jesus called us to die.

All brands of Christianity are centred around a cross.   Indeed, † is the most important Christian symbol.   It is found in every church, every Christian institution, almost every "Christian" home.   Many Christians even display it as a decorative item on their necklaces and key chains.   But it is, sadly, a fact that most have forgotten the meaning of the cross.   Jesus was nailed on a cross.   A cross represents sacrificial death.   Christians must seriously learn the meaning of taking up a cross!

Today, Christians are too preoccupied with saving their own lives.   But this is not what the gospel is about.   In *Mark* 8:35 we read, "For anyone who wants to save his (her) life will lose it; but anyone who loses his (her) life for my (Jesus) sake and for the sake of the gospel, will save it" (*Jerusalem Bible*).   It is refreshing to read about this "alternative" life style as advocated by the life and teaching of Jesus Christ, that people should live for others rather than live for themselves only.

Actually this is what people experience in their daily living. People have rice to eat because there are farmers who plant rice, plow the fields, irrigate them, then harvest the grain.   There are people who transport the rice to markets.   And finally, there are people who cook the rice.   A lot of people labour and sweat so that we can have a bowl of rice to eat.   We live because of sacrifices made by other people. Christians should be especially sensitive to this chain of self-giving.

Today, many in Hong Kong think only in terms of money, wealth, status, and privilege.   Few would think seriously about the deeper meaning of their life.   Hong Kong's citizens, especially Christians, need to be reminded what the Christian gospel is about: "What gain then is it for a man to win the whole world and ruin his life? And indeed what can a man offer in exchange for his life?" (*Mark* 8:37).

People in Hong Kong should relearn what "human dignity" involves, what it means to live a dignified life. People, Christians included, generally pursue their self-interests. They are prepared to kowtow to or kneel before those in power in order to achieve this goal. When Hong Kong's citizens criticize the business community for selling out Hong Kong to China, and Britain for adopting a policy of appeasement towards China on Hong Kong transition arrangements so that British commercial interests would be preserved, they should look at their own behaviour as well. In Hong Kong, where everyone looks at his/her short term interest, where greed is the dominant driving force in motivating people to work hard, it would be refreshing to hear once again, "There is more happiness in giving than in receiving" (*Acts* 20:35). This is the practical teaching of the early Church, that Christians should learn to give rather than be constantly thinking of receiving from others.

Before they try to evangelize other people, Hong Kong's Christians especially need to "evangelize" themselves first, meaning they must try to understand the gospel and its demands and implications. At a world mission and evangelism conference sponsored by the World Council of Churches, held in Melbourne, Australia, in May 1980, one of the major concerns was "self-evangelism." Christians throughout the world need to relearn what the gospel is about. Nowadays the brand of Christianity evangelical Christians try to propagate is a very different brand than that taught by the early Church. It is highly distorted. It is about "God's blessings on those who join the Church." But this is only one small part of the gospel. The whole of the gospel concerns the Church or Christians being channels of God's blessings (c.f. *Genesis* 12:1-3). The Church or Christians are God's servants in the world. Their constant concern is not what they can gain from this world; but, rather, what they can contribute to the development of this world so that it becomes more humane.

Training for Discipleship

Evangelism, or preaching the gospel, was the centre of the mission of the early Church. The goal of evangelism was to "make disciples."   Indeed, this was Jesus's commandment given to his disciples before he departed from them and ascended.   This, as recorded in the Gospel according to *Matthew*, "Go, therefore, make disciples of all nations, baptize them in the name of the Father and of the Son and of the Holy Spirit, and teach them to observe all the commandments I gave you" (28:19-20a).   This was later known as the Great Commission.

Contrary to what most Christians believe nowadays, the Great Commission is not about spreading the gospel; it is not about inviting neighbours, friends, and students to come to church meetings.   The Great Commission is about making disciples.   It is about the Church's efforts to train people to be Jesus's disciples.

Jesus's disciples are the people who have decided to follow Jesus, in word, in deed, and in life style.   Today, many Christians are nominal disciples.   They follow Jesus in name only, but not in any substantive way.   For example, Matthew tells us that "Jesus went around the whole of Galilee teaching in their synagogues, proclaiming the Good News of the Kingdom, and curing all kinds of diseases and sickness among the people" (*Matthew* 4:23, c.f. 9:35, Note 3).   These are the things Christians must do.

Christianity is not a religion concerned mainly with worship by its followers.   Christianity is a way of life.   That way of life was fully demonstrated by the life, ministry and death of Jesus Christ.   As Christians, in following Jesus, they should reflect on what Jesus said and did, as well as on his total life style.   Therefore, the Christian faith basically concerns faithfulness to Jesus.   Borrowing Cardinal Newman's terms, Christianity is much more than notional or intellectual assent, it is about **real assent** (Note 4), meaning Christianity requires of its followers total commitment.

What did Jesus do?   To begin with, the gospels *Matthew, Mark, Luke* and *John*, give many graphic and vivid descriptions about Jesus's ministry.   Jesus was busy all the time.   He went around helping people be full human beings: healing the sick, enlightening those looking for the meaning of life, and setting free the people who were suppressed.   Dietrich Bonhoeffer summed up Jesus's ministry with a simple phrase, Jesus was "the man for others."   Jesus came not for himself, but that others "may have life, and have it abundantly" (*John* 10:10, Revised Standard Version).

This is Jesus's self-understanding, "For the Son of Man himself did not come to be served but to serve, and to give his life as a ransom for many" (*Mark* 10:45, c.f. *Matthew* 20:28).

One of the most famous Christological hymns is *Philippians* 2:6-11 (Note 5).   The first part of the hymn was about Jesus's incarnation.

> His state was divine,
> yet he did not cling
> to his equality with God
> but emptied himself
> to assume the condition of a slave,
> and became as men are;
> he was humbler yet,
> even to accepting death,
> death on a cross.
>   (*Philippians* 2:6-8, *Jerusalem Bible*)

The content of this hymn is fairly simple.   It describes Jesus's high position (he was divine and equal to God), something beyond human experience and understanding.   But for the sake of human kind, he humbled himself.   Though he was full, he emptied himself and became a man --not an ordinary man, but a slave.   He gave up his life.   When he was killed he was nailed on a cross, together will two robbers.   He did not die heroically, but shamefully, alongside criminals.   As if this were not enough to describe Jesus's total humanity, the Apostles' Creed added the following words: "He was buried and descended into hell."

From the highest (divine), beyond human comprehension, to the lowest (hell), again beyond human comprehension, this was the way Jesus showed us the new life, a life of total service and commitment. As his disciples, Christians ought to reflect on this very seriously.

The Church is a fellowship of Christians. Christians gather together as a Church to try to give witness to the good news. But at the same time Christians gather to be trained, so that when they scatter, they can continue to witness the same in their work and in their home.

The major task, then, of any local church or congregation of Christians is to nurture Christians so that they are equipped to build up the "body of Christ" (*Ephesians* 4:15), the body of people who dare to do the Christ deed and speak the Christ word and to live a life-style of Christ.

The Church in Hong Kong is busy doing many things except training disciples. The early Church set a good example of what a Church should do to train its members. It preached (Kerygma), taught (Didache), did Christian service (Diakonia), and engaged in Christian fellowship (Kononia). Undergirding all these is Worship (Litourgia). Preaching and Christian service are the external mission of the Church. Fellowship and teaching are the Church's internal life. They are the four legs of a table, and that table is Worship. Without one, the table will collapse. Unfortunately, most of the local congregations in Hong Kong today do only two or three of these basic things.

The most important thing any Church does is Worship. The main purpose of Christian worship is to praise God, to magnify God's continuing work of creating, saving and sustaining. Christian worship should therefore not be confined to the sanctuary, it should be extended into the world. Worshipping God in a Church premise is important. But it is not an end in itself. It is a rehearsal of life. It should enable worshippers to continue their act of worship in their daily life.   Hence, the act of "sending forth" in any worship service is vital.   After a common worship, Christians are sent back into the world, into their work environment, and there they continue to praise God.   This means they must try to rid their world of the things which sully God's name, things such as hunger, poverty, racism and violence (Note 6).

Local churches in Hong Kong do not, as a rule, take these basics (Liturgia, Didache, Kononia, Diakonia and Kerygma) very seriously. Part of the problem lies in the fact that full-time pastors have been very poorly trained.   Many of them have not been exposed to the rich Christian tradition.   Most of them were never trained to have an analytical mind and to dare to make decisions which may run contrary to the thinking of their sheep, the members of the spiritual flocks churches are supposed to guide.

One of the most important things for the citizens of Hong Kong to learn is to rid themselves of the colonial mind-set, be able to stand up and live a dignified life.   The Church should act as a catalytic agent.   But since its pastors and seminary students were never trained to be independent, to think and act independently (Note 7), it is asking too much for them to lead the way.   The chairperson of the executive committee of a major denomination once commented that too many of the pastors in his church have "weak knees," which literally means they are not able to stand up and be counted.   Indeed, most church leaders in Hong Kong today seek to be popular especially among members of their own denomination, rather than to stand up on principle and be at odds with them.   For example, when it became fashionable to run exchange programmes with the Christians in China, few pastors dared to express openly that they had other priorities.   As a matter of fact, most of the "visits" to China and from China have become very superficial.   Activities are confined to eating, drinking and sight-seeing.   Very little genuine exchange of ideas takes place. While on previous visits, this author always tried to ask his counterparts about their experiences, sufferings, and reflections on the

Cultural Revolution, as well as what they thought of June 4. But he was astonished to discover that Chinese pastors did not want to share their feelings --even off the record.

In a way, all people suffer as a result of a more authoritarian rule. Everybody thinks the best way for survival is to be acquiescent. The more people are concerned, the more they are afraid. This gives the people who are on top even more power to dictate, to define and to limit the rights and freedom of ordinary citizens. But the Church must dare to stand up, challenge the viewpoint of the powerful, and put forth its viewpoint that all people are created equal. All human beings should enjoy certain basic rights, rights such as the freedom of thought, of expression, and the freedom from fear. These rights are God-given and inborn; they are not given at the mercy of the rulers.

Reconstructing Humanness

Men and women do not live by bread alone. As human beings, they must continue to strive for the most important attribute of humanness --dignity. Standing up and demanding a caring society is one way people can continuously improve on the quality of their lives.

The two creation accounts as found in *Genesis* 1 and 2 assert in no uncertain terms that human beings are not self-made. They are part of God's creation. As beings created by God, they bear God's image. This means that every human being must mirror God as God is made known through God's acts in both the Old and the New Testaments (Note 8). God continues to act in history. God's acts of creation, salvation, and sustenance all continue. Humans, Christians especially, should actively participate in these saving acts. In fact, after God created people in God's own image, God commanded:

> Be fruitful, multiply, fill the earth and conquer it.
> BE MASTERS of the fish of the sea, the birds of heaven and
> all living animals on the earth.
>
> (*Genesis* 1:28, *Jerusalem Bible*)

The words "Be Masters" here mean two things: a) under God's command, all people are the Subjects of this planet earth, and b) every human life is precious and ought to be respected.

Every person is a subject and not an object, like a tool or a machine which is used by other people.   Exploitation of people of any kind is a direct violation of God's will.   To put it another way, as subjects, people are actors, rather than objects to be acted upon.

Genesis 2:15 put the whole idea across even more succinctly, "God took the man and settled him in the garden of Eden to cultivate and to take care of it."   The garden of Eden is equivalent to the whole creation which includes all human beings living in it.   In other words, human beings have been given the responsibility to care, not only for themselves, but for others, and indeed for the world as a whole.

Every human life is precious and must be fully respected.   A sense of respect and care for all people, especially the weak and the young, serves as the basis of modern democracy.   True democracy means more than a form of government institution, it means a fundamental belief that every human life is precious and that everyone has a solemn responsibility to take care of each other.   Hence, to mind only one's own business is the biggest contradiction to democracy.

One of the most important developments of the 20th century has been that, due to the technology and information explosions, more and more people have become aware that the external authority or force which used to guide them has gradually broken down.   At last, it seems a greater possibility that people are in charge of their own futures and destinies.   People have come of age.   They have become aware of their basic rights, as well as social roles and responsibilities. People's quest for more democracy, freedom, human rights protection, and a fairer distribution of wealth have become the order of the day. This world trend is irreversible.   For example, many of the authoritarian governments in Asia tried to boost economic progress in their own countries, but at the same time tried to suppress their citizens' basic economic, social, cultural, civil and political rights.   But there have not been any success stories among them.

It is from this perspective that there may be cause for optimism in regards to China.   When Mao Zedong and Deng Xiaoping ruled China (1949-1976 and 1978-1997 respectively), they ruled it with an iron first.   But Jiang Zemin does not enjoy the same authority as did Mao and Deng, "liberators" of their homeland and key figures in the establishment of the People's Republic of China.   It is impossible to be authoritarian without that aura of historical legitimacy.   That being the case, Jiang has to rely on the PLA, as well as Chinese people for support.   Like it or not, Jiang will have to answer the people's calls for more freedom and increasing improvement of the quality of their lives. That means more liberalization, more economic as well as political reforms.

This suggests a great opportunity for the Church in Hong Kong, the Church in China, as well as the World Church to help build a more humane and caring global community.   The Church should advocate and promote a more open society, and should actively participate in and support democratic efforts throughout the world.   But first, the Universal Church throughout the world has to repent.   For too long, and far too often, churches not only sided with the ruling authorities, but also made great efforts to justify what the powerful regimes did. For example, in the 1930s the main body of the German Church sided with the Nazi regime.   In the 1960s many mainline churches in South Africa took the side of the apartheid regime and justified what it did.

But, with or without the Church's contribution, the whole world moves on.   Every country is moving towards a more citizen-oriented society.   Hong Kong may be the only exception.   There are enough signs showing that the citizens' civil and political rights are rolling back, bit by bit.   That being the case, sooner or later the social and economic rights of Hong Kong's citizens will also diminish.

This is the moment that the Church in Hong Kong should get its act together and respond.   It must not be a bystander.   It must not remain apathetic like the crowds, because, as the body of Christ, the Church should care.

In facing powerful authorities, it is always difficult for anybody to express his or her concerns.   In some instances, the institutional church leaders may think that it is in everyone's interest if the Church works with the authorities, and does whatever the authorities expect it to do.   But there are others within the Church who think that the Church should be prophetic, be critical of the decision makers who often make decisions only to enhance the interests of a small segment in the community, but overlook the interests and well-being of the masses.   Whatever the differences of opinion and approach, it is hoped that nobody within the Church in Hong Kong will turn to betraying one another for the sake of pleasing those in authority.   It is hoped that whatever happened in Jesus's time as recorded in the Gospel according to *John*, Chapter 13, and happened time and again in China as well as in many countries in Eastern Europe (Note 9), will not happen in Hong Kong.

This is a critical period for Hong Kong and China both.   China needs Hong Kong not because it is a goose which lays golden eggs, but because Hong Kong can help China in two crucial aspects: to be more modern and to be more involved in the international community. But in order that Hong Kong can help China, China must give Hong Kong enough space to maneuver.   China should adopt a "live and let live" attitude towards Hong Kong.   Hong Kong's citizens, and especially the Church in Hong Kong, should continuously communicate to China this very important point.

Within Hong Kong's society, for too long, the distribution of power and wealth has been extremely uneven.   Less than 10% of the citizens are at the top, enjoying probably more than 90% of the say (voice), while the 90% who constitute the masses get only the remaining 10%.   The privileges which Hong Kong's elites enjoy are phenomenal.   This disparity needs to be redressed.

Fortunately, as more and more young people become better educated, and more and more consider Hong Kong as their home (Note 10), they have awakened to the fact that they must contribute something for the betterment of the society as a whole, not just their place within it. The Church in Hong Kong must seize this golden opportunity to stimulate young people, especially those within the Church, to think more independently, thus broadening their social concerns. The Church can and should hasten the process of interaction between the "haves" and the "have-nots."

The Church in Hong Kong is a young one, but it is a part of the Universal Church. Through their support for it, members of the Universal Church have an important role to play in determining Hong Kong's future.

Unfortunately, overseas churches are hesitant to act. Oftentimes, it is argued, this is because they have to wait for the signal from their "partners" in Hong Kong, meaning the denominational headquarters, the Hong Kong Christian Council, and the like.

A lesson must be learned from the case of Romania. During Ceausescu's totalitarian rule, the dictator was well supported by the church leaders in his country. Most of the overseas churches, including the World Council of Churches, throughout those years supported the institutional churches in Romania, rather than the suffering people within those congregations (Note 11).

Churches throughout the world must discern the different voices in Hong Kong, recognizing especially the voices of those who **care** for Hong Kong's overall development; of those who **care** for the well being of the masses rather than the privileged few; of those who **dare** to speak up **honestly**.

Concerned overseas churches should keep a close watch on Hong Kong, be a friend to those who have the courage to speak with their hearts, so that they may feel that they are not alone. The struggle in Hong Kong is by no means a losing battle.   As long as a small group of concerned people does not give up, but remains persistent in pressing for social concerns, the impossible will become possible.

This, indeed, is the Hong Kong spirit.   Hong Kong has, time and again, gone through extremely difficult moments.   But because of its citizens' resilience, Hong Kong overcame all these problems.   An economic miracle was created.

The first ever Olympic gold medal won by Hong Kong went to Li Lai Shan, a female wind-surfer.   When Li was interviewed about her feelings prior to the medals ceremony, she commented that people should know that not all the sports men and women in Hong Kong are garbage.   The background for this special comment was the fact that her first European trainer quit, saying that he should not waste any more time on Li.   Many times subsequently, Li had thought of giving up.   But she decided not to.   She worked even harder than before. Finally, came her success.

The successive fall of Eastern European regimes in 1989 -- beginning with Romania in October and ending with East Germany in December-- was another miracle.   There were many factors involved. But one of the least notable ones was the fact that in those countries, throughout the past four and a half decades, many Church people, artists, and intellectuals had refused to give up.   They held the view that doing something is always better than doing nothing.   They kept on broadcasting the ideas of democracy.   When the opportunity came in each context, many people rose up.

Hong Kong's home nursing program is another example of how success can be achieved through the tenacity of a few.   Meant as an experiment to help solve the hospital bed shortage in the 1960s, the home nursing program grew to be a a key component of health care in Hong Kong thanks to the hard work of a few people.

In 1968, seven women were recruited to take care of a bed-ridden stroke patient in his home (which was half of a cubicle in a resettlement block). Each took turns, spending one and a half hours daily to give him medicine, help him exercise, bathe him, and do all sorts of household chores. This experiment prompted the establishment of the home nursing program, first started by Yang Social Service Centre, and later implemented by the United Christian Hospital. By the mid-1970s, it had become a full-fledged service subvented by the Hong Kong government. These seven Christian women, who were old and not well-educated, but who were willing to contribute what little they had --their love and concern-- became the pioneers of an important health care program in Hong Kong.

Miracles do happen when people are persistent and decide to contribute whatever they have.

In the Old Testament, we often read about Isaiah's prophecy that one day the Israelites would "make roads in the wilderness and rivers in the desert" (*Isaiah* 43:19; c.f. *Isaiah* 35:6 and 41:18). In 1966, when this author visited Palestine, he saw only wilderness and desert; but when he returned in 1976, he saw kibbutz after kibbutz; he saw many new roads and plantations. The people there worked extraordinarily hard to make these things happen. The impossible was made possible.

In Jesus's healing of an epileptic, as recorded in *Mark* 8:15-29, his disciples asked Jesus why they themselves had failed to drive out the demons. Jesus replied, "Everything is possible for anyone who has faith" (8:23).

In times of radical change, the Church of Jesus Christ in Hong Kong is called upon to manifest this kind of faith in God.

160 A Church In Transition

NOTES

1. Most of these evangelical congregations are affiliated with the Baptist Church, the Christian Alliance Church, the Evangel Church and hundreds of independent congregations. Some of the mainline churches are also oriented toward evangelism. The Church of Christ in China Wanchai Church and its seven off-shoots are good examples.

2. Quite a few examples are found in the *Acts of the Apostles* in the Apostolic preaching, namely the Apostle Peter's preaching, found in *Acts* 2:14-40; 3:12-26; 4:9-12; 5:29-32 and 10:34-43; or in the Apostle Paul's preaching, as found in *Acts* 13:16-41.

3. 4:23 and 9:35 are known as summary statements in *Matthew*.

4. John Henry Cardinal Newman's book on the "Grammar of Assent" (published by Doubleday in 1955) gave detailed analyses of Notional and Real Assent. See especially Chapter 4.

5. In the New Testament, there are several Christological Hymns or Hymns of Praise for Christ, viz., *Philippians* 2:6-11, *Ephesians* 1:15-23; *Colossians* 1:15-20; I Peter 3:18-22; *Hebrews* 1:1-4.

6. The racial genocide which happened in Croatia, part of the former Yugoslavia, and the thousands of refugees who continue to die of hunger in Zaire, certainly contradict God's will, and greatly distort God's total creation.

7. The quality of seminary education in Hong Kong is, on the whole, fairly poor. Part of the reason for this is the fact that these institutions lack resources, human as well as financial. There are far too many seminaries and Bible schools in Hong Kong, 17 altogether. Every denomination wants to do its own thing. They are not prepared to pull their rather strained resources together. Moreover, Churches in Hong Kong

consider their preachers and pastors as managers, rather than leaders.   They do not expect too much from their pastors. Pastors are never considered professionals, like medical doctors or clinical psychologists.   As a result, their training falls far below that of professionals.

8.   In his book, *God Who Acts: Biblical Theology as Recital* (published by SCM Press in 1952), G. Ernest Wright argues that the God is the God who works in human history. Consequently, all of history becomes *Heilsgeschichte*, or the Saving History.

9.   *John* 13 recorded Judas's betrayal of Jesus.   In the midst of a meal (the Last Supper), Jesus quoted the Old Testament by saying there was "one who has lifted up his heel against me" (13:18, direct quote from Ps. 41:9, meaning "someone who shares my table betrays me").   In China, during the political upheavals in the 1950s, and especially during the Cultural Revolution between 1966 and 1976, there were countless cases indicating that pastors and lay leaders turned against each other in order to save their own skins.

10.   Many of Hong Kong's citizens of the older generations consider Hong Kong as their place of sojourn rather than their permanent home.   They came to Hong Kong to earn a living.

11.   The WCC, after the fall of Nicolae Ceausescu, did reflect on the whole matter in its Central Committee meeting held in March 1990.   A participant, Karoly Toth (from the Reformed Church in Hungry), commented in the discussion that WCC must not confuse the Church with the church leadership.   This is a somber reminder for the Universal Church.

APPENDIX I

THE FAITH SUSTAINED BY HONG KONG CHRISTIANS IN CONTEMPORARY SOCIAL AND POLITICAL CHANGES

Drafted on April 16, 1984, by a group of Evangelical Christians, regarding the Future of the Church.
Translated by Alison Lee.

Introduction

The emergence of the "97 Issue" has produced a great shock in Hong Kong, causing fear and restlessness among the general public. Being the people of God, we feel the need at the present time to re-affirm the faith which the Church has been upholding, and to look for our particular role and mission in this time of historical transition for the purpose of finding the future direction of witness for the Church. Having had a few discussion meetings under the direction of the Grace of God, we have reached the following ten common understandings of faith, to be put forward for reference by the congregations:

I.   Our Views on Social and Political Changes
    We affirm that God is the Lord who creates, redeems, adjudicates and controls the development of history; therefore, we believe any changes in the future of Hong Kong are under His care. Since we have had such faith, we will not waiver, but with peace of mind will work hard to accomplish what He wishes be done to us.

At the same time, being Hong Kong citizens, we have the responsibility to make use of the wisdom bestowed by God to objectively analyze the changes in history, face reality, and actively take up the responsibilities expected of Christians in this time of historic change.

II.   The Principle of the Unchanging Church in the Midst of Social Changes

Under whatever social and political circumstances, we should take the Bible as the highest principle of our faith, life and commitment.

In times of social upheaval, we are bound to feel an impact, to face temptations or even to experience weaknesses. Therefore, we recognize that, under whatever circumstances, we have to be faithful to Christ, not to compromise because of the changes in the environment; nor to sacrifice the principles of the biblical truth out of strategic considerations. Relying on the might of the Lord, we should hold steadfastly the covenant we made with our Lord, to follow His commands with absolute obedience and to witness the Lord in times of crises in order that His name can be glorified.

III.   The Nature and Mission of the Church

We believe the Church is the concrete body of spiritual people called by God through the gospel in the name of Jesus Christ.

The Church is the body of Christ, filled with His spirit. God established the Church to glorify His name on earth, to serve the people, to witness and to extend the Kingdom of God in order to accomplish God's will to create and redeem through Christ. These ends are to be actualized through the following functions:

(i)   through preaching about the gospel of God's redemption locally and to the world;

(ii)   through worship, fellowship, pastoral work and spiritual discipline, to develop the spiritual life of believers;

(iii)   through being the light and salt of the world, promoting the renewal of society and culture.

This mission is given to the Church by Christ. Therefore, under whatever environmental changes, the Church should do its utmost to preserve the totality of this mission, neither letting it be deluded by the will of men or political influence, nor fragmented.

IV.   Christians' Responsibilities for and Expectations of Hong Kong

As a portion of Hong Kong's citizenry, we recognize that Christians, together with other citizens, have the responsibility to shape Hong Kong's future, making it a democratic and lawful society which respects human rights, freedom and equality, and is stable and prosperous.   At this moment of historical transition, we should shoulder the responsibility of spreading the gospel to Hong Kong people, so that they can enjoy the grace of God and live a holistic life.

We have the expectation that after 1997 Hong Kong can maintain a high degree of autonomous rule.   We also expect that citizens can enjoy their God-given human rights, including freedom of speech, association, country, religion as well as the freedom to preach, etc., so that Hong Kong can make positive contributions to the overall modernization and democratization of China.

V.   Hong Kong Christians' Commitment to China

Being Chinese, we are closely related to the fate and history of all people in China.

Therefore, we should not only care about what benefits Hong Kong's people, but, under the principles of the Bible, care about and participate in the construction of China.   We expect people in China will fully enjoy the human rights and freedoms given by God, so that China can become a country with justice being done and people living a prosperous life.   We also wish to have more Chinese people come to know God the Creator, and enjoy His grace and redemption.   To these ends we are willing to do our very best.

VI.   Relationship between Hong Kong Churches and the Ecumenical Church

We believe that Hong Kong churches are part of the Ecumenical Church, being spiritually linked with churches all over the world.

Therefore, we should maintain communication with one another, helping one another to develop and to shoulder together the mission of the Gospel.

We confirm that The Hong Kong churches and the churches in China and in the world possess spiritually the same origin.   At the same time, we recognize the localization of the churches.   Therefore, with the background of Chinese culture, and under the peculiar circumstances of Hong Kong, the Hong Kong churches should work hard to exert the uniqueness of the local congregations and maintain their autonomy and independence in administrative structure and, at the same time, participate positively in the preaching work all over the world.

VII. Our Views on the Relationship between the Church and the State
We believe the authority of the government comes from God. We should be obedient to the government under the relevant terms of reference to government authority.   When the demands of the government are in contradiction to the will of God, however, we should instead follow the working principle of obeying God.   The authority of the government has its definite sphere.   The functions of the government as given by God are to maintain law and order, stabilize society, and ensure the security of people's livelihood. Accordingly, under the rule of the constitution, the government should be responsible to the people.   Christians in society should play the role of the prophet, and actively urge the government to act out justice for the benefit of the people.

VIII. Social Change and the Church's Renewal From Within
We recognize that in the past decades, the Church has attained certain achievements in establishing local congregations, schools and social services.   Nevertheless, we have to admit that we have not been sharp-sighted in our response to the metamorphic changes in Hong · Kong society.   Nor has there been any breakthrough in the model of the Church.   In this moment of historical changes, the Church should engage in deep reflection and search for renewal to turn crises into

opportunities. The following are some important points for consideration:

(i)   strengthening knowledge about the development of past history and the present environment;

(ii)   delivering that message which is appropriate to the contemporary, and being faithful to the truth;

(iii)   paying attention to the establishment of faith and the actualization of love in the spiritual preparation for the believers;

(iv)   strengthening the training of discipleship;

(v)   exerting the influence of preachers and church leaders as role models;

(vi)   setting up appropriate models of the Church and models of commitment.

IX.   The Witness of Christian Unity

In an era of change, the Church, because of external pressure and internal discord, is facing the crisis of segregation. Therefore, during this time, we must recognize the unity of Christians in Christ, accept one another on the basis of common belief, and trust one another. Notwithstanding different view points, Christians must communicate with each other to try and find concrete proposals of cooperation, to support each other, to complement each other, and to stand up to face challenges together.

X.   Church's Self Preservation and Loyalty

In hopes of the Lord's return, we should maintain the Church's chastity and be faithful to the Lord, guarding against the infiltration of secularism or any influence of those in power. Furthermore, we must love one other in Christ, and establish the body of Christ to glorify God's name.

Conclusion

During this important time of great social change, we have to be particularly eager to work hard in getting opportunities to spread the gospel and witness Christ.   In recognizing the above points, we have experienced deeply our own weaknesses, knowing too well that we cannot rely on our own strength and determination to stand up in the midst of impacts and challenges.   Therefore, we depend on the might and faithfulness of our God, the tender love of Christ, and the presence of the Holy Spirit, to guard our faith and to lead us on the road ahead.

APPENDIX II

THE MANIFESTO ON RELIGIOUS FREEDOM

Introduction

On August 31, 1984, "A Manifesto of the Protestant Churches in Hong Kong on Religious Freedom," together with a list of Christian organizations supporting the manifesto, was sent to the Chinese Government and the British Government through the New China News Agency and the Government Secretariat, respectively. It is hoped that, in drafting the Basic Law and in carrying out the policy regarding religion after 1997, consideration and respect will be given to religious freedom, which has been enjoyed by the churches in Hong Kong for over a hundred years.

The drafting of the manifesto has taken about half a year. Over a hundred Christians from different denominations and theological traditions have been consulted. At the same time, about 100 well known church leaders signed an open appeal to Christian denominational bodies; 200 churches, 5 theological seminaries and 44 Christian organizations and groups have responded and supported the manifesto.

A MANIFESTO OF THE PROTESTANT CHURCH IN HONG KONG ON RELIGIOUS FREEDOM

At this critical moment of historical change, the Protestant Church in Hong Kong wishes to express its deepest concern about the future of religious freedom in Hong Kong and to make the following statement:

Religious freedom and the openness of a society always go hand in hand. Religious freedom is a sign of social progress. We believe that genuine religious freedom must be based on the human rights which God bestows on all people at birth, and that therefore it is the responsibility of all governments to protect religious freedom.

Whether religious freedom is protected depends on how the society concerned looks at human rights, which include the freedoms of thought, expression, peaceful assembly and association, movement, etc.   We are convinced that genuine religious freedom can only exist in a society that respects human rights.

Religious freedom has been and still is part and parcel of the rights the people of Hong Kong are enjoying and exercising.   As far as the Protestant Church in Hong Kong is concerned, at present religious freedom in concrete terms means the rights and freedoms to do the following:

I.   Personal
1.   to choose religious belief without being subject to social discrimination and deprivation of civil rights,
2.   to choose denomination, theological position and liturgy,
3.   to purchase and to possess religious books and magazines,
4.   to propagate religious beliefs.

II.   Family
1.   to allow one's young children to be baptized and participate in other religious rites in accordance with one's religious tradition,
2.   to conduct worship and religious education at home,
3.   to hold religious ceremonies for one's family members on occasions such as birth, marriage, funeral, etc.

III.   Church
1.   Assembly
a.   to host religious activities at different times and venues, such as worship services, prayer meetings, Sunday schools, fellowships, conferences, Bible-study classes, crusades, baptism classes, revival meetings, baptisms, etc.,

b.   to have legal access to public facilities for evangelism and spiritual nurture gatherings such as crusades, revival meetings, dramas, concerts, etc.,

c.   to organize and support Christian fellowships for believers in various professions for evangelism and spiritual nurture purposes.

2.   Evangelism and spiritual nurture

a.   to use electronic media such as movies, radio, gramophone records, recording tapes, video tapes, slides, etc., for the production and broadcast of evangelism and spiritual nurture programmes,

b.   to publish and distribute Bibles, hymnals, prayer books, journals, books, teaching materials, tracts, etc.,

c.   to lead people at various ages to Christ by preaching to and teaching them content of the Christian faith.

3.   Service and witness

a.   to set up social welfare/service and medical service agencies as expression of the Church's holistic concern for the community and the individual,

b.   to run educational institutions such as kindergartens, primary and secondary schools, post-secondary colleges, vocational training schools, etc.,

c.   to set up agencies that monitor and participate in the making of public policies, protection of people's livelihood and eradication of social injustices, as an expression of the Church's holistic concern for the community and the individual.

4.   Human and other resources

a.   to accept, manage, use and keep donations and endowments from sources inside and outside Hong Kong for religious and social service purposes,

b.   to establish and maintain links and to share resources with individuals and church organizations inside and outside Hong Kong under the principle of mutual respect,

c.   to run theological seminaries and research centres for academic research and man-power training purposes,

d.   to employ and ordain clergy in accordance with denominational traditions.

5   Organization and management

a.   to decide on organizational structure and to set membership qualifications and requirements according to denominational traditions and constitution,

b.   to (in the case of both local churches and overseas missionary bodies, and in compliance with the law) acquire, manage and use properties such as churches, parsonages, offices, schools, hospitals, socials service centres, retreat centres, etc.,

c.   to own and run cemeteries.

6   Others

to engage in other legitimate work not mentioned above, but related to the Church.

The above is a rough description of the activities of the Church and of how religious freedom is understood and actualized in Hong Kong. We earnestly hope that the Church in Hong Kong will be able to enjoy and exercise these rights and freedoms after 1997.

We believe that Christians should commit themselves to the maintenance and development of a society that respects human rights. Christians in Hong Kong have the responsibility to make Hong Kong a place where people will continue to live in freedom, stability and prosperity even after its sovereignty reverts to China. They also have the duty to champion the cause of human rights and democracy, and thus to contribute to the future happiness of the Chinese people.

As the Church is a symbol of the presence of God in this world, we reiterate that at this moment of historical change, we are with the people of Hong Kong in the struggle to strengthen our society. We call on all Christians to work with one mind for a better future for

Hong Kong; to be salt and light; to manifest God's love, peace and justice; to serve the needy and the weak; to console the injured; to fulfill our responsibilities to the community, the nation and the people; and to complete the mission God has given us, helping everyone understand the gospel and live according to God's will.

Selected Bibliography

On Hong Kong's Political Transition:

The Future of Hong Kong. *The Annals of the American Academy of Political and Social Science.* Max J. Skidmore, special editor. September 1996.

The Other Hong Kong Report. Volumes 1-9 (1989-1997). Various editors. Hong Kong: The Chinese University Press.

Lane, Kevin P. *Sovereignty and the Status Quo: The Historical Roots of China's Hong Kong Policy.* Boulder: Westview Press, 1990.

Wang Enbao. *Hong Kong 1997: The Politics of Transition.* Boulder: L. Rienner, 1995.

On the Church in Hong Kong:

Brown, Deborah. *Turmoil in Hong Kong on the Eve of Communist Rule: The Fate of the Church.* San Francisco: Mellen Research University Press, 1993.

Coulson, Gail V. *The Enduring Church: Christians in China and Hong Kong.* New York: Friendship Press, 1996.

Kwok Nai-wang. *1997: Hong Kong's Struggle for Selfhood.* Hong Kong: DAGA Press, 1996.

Lee, Peter K. H. "Hong Kong: Living in the Shadow of the Third World." In *Asian Christian Spirituality: Reclaiming Traditions.* Virginia Fabella, Peter K. H. Lee and David Kwang-sun Suh, eds. Maryknoll, NY: Orbis Books, 1992: 106-120.

Leung, Beatrice, ed. *Church & State Relations in 21st Century Asia.* Hong Kong: The University of Hong Kong Press, 1996.

Smith, Carl T. *Chinese Christians: Elites, Middlemen, and the Church in Hong Kong.* Hong Kong: Oxford University Press, 1985.

Vikner, David. *The Role of Christian Missions in the Establishment of Hong Kong's System of Education.* Ann Arbor, MI: The University of Michigan Press, 1996.

HONG KONG CHRISTIAN INSTITUTE

Founded by 120 leading Hong Kong Christians in 1988, HKCI attempts to gather Christians together and enable them to make a contribution to the social betterment of Hong Kong, especially during the crucial transitional period leading to the transfer of Hong Kong's sovereignty to China on June 30, 1997.

HKCI is engaged in:
1. Being a social critic
   -doing social analysis
   -contributing to the of a democratic culture
2. Being an educator
   -organizing courses and seminars
   -publishing a bi-monthly theological journal *Reflection*
   -publishing four series of books on
   > Church and Society
   > Faith and Life
   > Contemporary Interpretation of the Bible
   > Civic Education
   -publishing study materials
   > civic education packages for high schools
   > study guides on political awareness for church groups
3. Being a member of the Ecumenical Movement which is concerned with building a just, participatory, and sustainable civil society.

You are invited to be a friend of HKCI. Just send your name and address to 11 Mongkok Road, 10th Floor, Kowloon, Hong Kong. You will receive a four-page monthly newsletter on Hong Kong issues form its Director.

HKCI depends on support from a network of friends. Prayers, ideas and financial contributions are always welcome.

WE NEED YOUR SUPPORT

I would like to support Hong Kong Christian Institute in the following ways:

☐ Include HKCI in my daily prayers.

☐ I wish to become an Associate Member of HKCI (Please fill in the attached Associate Members Application Form)

☐ I wish to donate $ _____ to HKCI.

☐ I wish to introduce the following friends to HKCI, please put them into HKCI's mailing list.

_____

_____

Name: (Ms./Mr./Rev.) _____

Address: _____

_____

Telephone: _____

Occupation: _____

Notes:

1. Please complete the above form and return it with your payment of donation to the Hong Kong Christian Institute, 11 Mongkok Road, 10/F., Kowloon, Hong Kong (Tel: 2398-1699 / Fax: 2787-4765)

2. Cheques should be crossed to "Hong Kong Christian Institute" and if the cheque is not in Hong Kong Dollars, bank exchange charges of HK$60.00 should be added.

APPLICATION FOR ASSOCIATE MEMBER

Name: (Ms./Mr./Rev.) _____

Chinese Name (if applicable): _____

Occupation: _____

School / Education Level: _____

Church Affiliation: _____

Telephone No. _____ (office)_____ (home)

Facsimile: _____ Email: _____

Correspondence Address: _____

_____

I support the objective and functions of the HKCI and apply to join the Institute as an associate member. I am enclosing my membership fee / donation in the amount of _____

Applicant's Signature: _____

Office use only _____

Cash / Cheque No. _____ Membership No. _____

Notes:

1. Applicants please complete the above form and return it with your payment of membership fee / donation to the Hong Kong Christian Institute, 11 Mongkok Road, 10/F., Kowloon, Hong Kong.

2. Cheques should be crossed to "Hong Kong Christian Institute" and if the cheque is not in Hong Kong Dollars, bank exchange charges of HK$60.00 should be added.

3. Associate membership fee: local HK$100 / Overseas HK$200 (or equivalent) / 50% discount for full-time students.